Allyship Actually

Why it's 'We' and not 'Me'

Allyship Actually
Why it's 'We' and not 'Me'

LUCY GRIMWADE

AND

DAVID BARROW

IT Governance Publishing

IT Governance Publishing Ltd
Unit 3, Clive Court
Bartholomew's Walk
Cambridgeshire Business Park
Ely, Cambridgeshire
CB7 4EA
United Kingdom
www.itgovernancepublishing.co.uk

First published in the United Kingdom in 2024 by IT Governance Publishing.

ISBN 978-1-78778-529-8

Cover image originally sourced from Vecteezy.

ACKNOWLEGEMENTS

We would like to thank the following individuals for their help and support during the production of this book:

- Vicki Utting – managing executive of IT Governance Publishing;
- Susanna Beard – author;
- Sophie Hussey – director of Lapis Consulting Services Ltd.;
- Matt Beran – Ticket Volume podcast host and product marketing geek at InvGate;
- Michelle Major-Goldsmith – consultant, accredited trainer, speaker;
- Nicola Day – publications manager at IT Governance Publishing; and
- Kirsty Ridge – copy editor at GRC International Group PLC and freelance copy editor.

DISCLAIMER

The issues raised in this book might be upsetting for some readers. For more information about the issues discussed, and links to reputable organisations that offer support and advice related to these subjects, please visit the resources section at the end of the book.

The content of this book is based on real events. Names, locations and job titles may have been changed to protect and anonymise identities of the people involved.

PREFACE

This isn't one of those leadership books that you pick up off the shelf or 'buy now' from Amazon, then leave on your coffee table or by your bedside for the next two years before 'gifting' it to the charity shop. We see you and we know that you do this; we are both that person too. So, no judgement here.

We didn't want to write a management guide, we wanted to write something that gives us a voice, and we hope it gives you the confidence to use your voice too.

This book comprises a series of short stories. Real stories, by real people. People that you might be interacting with on a daily basis. We have, of course, tailored and edited scenarios to protect both ourselves and those whom we write about. What you are about to read is based on our truths. Some events have been slightly adjusted or exaggerated for impact, but always remember that they are based on true stories.

There are two lead characters: Lucy and David. They are joined by an array of other characters, some of whom are contributors. We have villains, naturally – but we don't have a hero. In essence, allyship is the hero of these stories.

We are not experts, and we are not fiction writers.

We are, however, storytellers.

For both of us, it has been a gift to have others around us who have been willing to share their experiences. Thank you to all our contributors.

Doing this project has given us an opportunity for our friendship to flourish. How odd, a male and a female who have become true friends (we say this tongue in cheek).

We hope this book helps you to overcome challenges or think a bit differently.

But most importantly, we hope that you become an ally to all.

Why it's about 'We' and not 'Me'

As explained, this novel is a selection of character driven real-life stories, experiences that neither author could tell as 'me' but that make sense when viewed through the lens of 'we'.

Real stories can be entertaining and informative at the same time, however as authors we have taken the decision to switch from our 'fictional' world after our story 'ends' to the real world, with personal accounts written by our fantastic contributors included in the appendix at the end of the book. Everyone deserves a voice and in these cases we wanted these voices to be heard loud and clear.

Allyship Actually – Why it's 'We' not 'Me'.

FROM THE MOUTHS OF BABES

How do today's children feel about equality and allyship?

Betsy, aged six

Betsy has the attitude of a post-punk Vivienne Westwood, and we are all here for it. She has many girlfriends and thinks boys and girls are treated differently. She thinks boys get more to play with, and she thinks girls should be treated the same.

Betsy wants to be a farmer when she grows up, because she believes that girls can be farmers too.

Betsy wants everyone to be treated better, regardless of being a boy or girl or their skin colour.

Bradley, aged ten

Bradley has double the emotional intelligence of your average 25-year-old male.

Bradley already sees that boys and girls are treated differently. He says boys are not nice to girls, which makes him sad. He wants to help boys and girls get on.

He believes that because boys and girls are in the same classes, they should get the same opportunities. Bradley likes to help those less fortunate than him, no matter where they come from. You can often find him taking his pennies and passing them to the homeless and those raising money for charity. Bradley wants to be a footballer and he sees no reason why girls cannot be footballers too.

CONTENTS

Introduction..1
Chapter 1: The central characters 3
Chapter 2: The start of IT...................................11
Chapter 3: The first job.......................................19
Chapter 4: The job description............................29
Chapter 5: The interviews...................................37
Chapter 6: The other side of the table 47
Chapter 7: The bird in IT....................................53
Chapter 8: The job offer/rejection 59
Chapter 9: The first day......................................69
Chapter 10: In da club...75
Chapter 11: Horrible bosses 83
Chapter 12: Tales of real-world allyship 89
Chapter 13: Why so biased? 95
Chapter 14: Horrible bosses 2 109
Chapter 15: Feeling stuck 115
Chapter 16: Handling 'IT' 121
Chapter 17: B*tch..125
Chapter 18: Are men saying the wrong things?..........131
Chapter 19: Are we still experiencing this?................137
Chapter 20: The offsite meeting 143
Chapter 21: Stalker..151
Chapter 22: The Christmas party 163
Chapter 23: Imposter syndrome.......................177
Chapter 24: Cultural differences......................183
Chapter 25: She helps him 193
Chapter 26: I want to quit.................................201
Chapter 27: Always on; always anxious 207
Chapter 28: Can anyone help? 217
Chapter 29: Enough is enough..........................225

Contents

Chapter 30: The introduction 231
Chapter 31: Self-employed and self-sufficient 237
Chapter 32: Did you go shopping? 243
Chapter 33: Thank you, next 251
Chapter 34: Friendships 257
Chapter 35: 2024 and beyond 265
Chapter 36: The power skills 271
Chapter 37: Let's write a book 277
Chapter 38: New beginnings 283
Chapter 39: Allyship Actually 287
Appendix: Through their voices 293
About the authors – Who we really are 321
Resources 329
Further reading 335

INTRODUCTION

In and around the bustling heart of London, a city as rich in diversity as it is steeped in history, the interconnected lives of two seemingly unconnected individuals converge in a tale of modern allyship and personal growth. *Allyship Actually* weaves a story of mentorship, growth, and the power of standing together against the odds – reminding us that sometimes, the most pivotal allyships are forged out of coincidences, or is it fate?

Allyship Actually follows the narratives of Lucy, beginning her journey as a spirited newcomer to the tech industry and David, a seasoned tech professional who is always considering a bold leap into entrepreneurship, as their paths and those of a cast of characters cross in unexpected ways amid the backdrop of London's vibrant chaos.

David, having spent decades in the industry, has seen it all but is still taken aback by the subtle complexities of allyship that emerge in his later career. His journey is unknowingly ignited by a chance encounter with Lucy at Browns, the strip club and a fleeting, if awkward, moment at a Christmas party. These encounters, brief yet impactful, lay the groundwork for a connection that is later solidified through a professional introduction on LinkedIn.

Lucy, ten years David's junior and new to the tech world, faces the daily grind with a mix of fierce determination and naivety about the challenges that lie ahead. Her experiences with sexism in the workplace echo the struggles that many women face in male-dominated industries, but her resolve only strengthens as she navigates these trials. A mutual connection on LinkedIn throws Lucy and David together, and what follows is a transformative journey for both.

Together, David and Lucy navigate the intricacies of the working and real worlds, confronting personal and professional challenges. Through moments of mentorship, mutual support, and shared experiences at office gatherings and unexpected meetings, they discover that allyship is not just about supporting others in their battles but also about learning, growing, and finding common ground in the fight for a fairer, more equitable world.

CHAPTER 1: THE CENTRAL CHARACTERS

Lucy

Independent of mind and thought, Lucy is a successful professional with a toolkit of skills that makes the difficult look easy. Lucy's skills and mindset are forged from adversity; whether males are speaking over her, she's being ignored in meetings or she's accused of playing 'dressing up' at work, Lucy has formed a granite exterior – until she lets you in.

Lucy is the person you want in your corner, the definition of an ally. She has blazed a trail that sees her coaching leaders, public speaking and influencing this male-dominated world. It hasn't always been that way – from the start, Lucy had a difficult childhood both at home and at school.

David

David is working class, in his mid-40s and still learning. He has had a successful career but realises he could and should do better. What David lacks in education, he makes up for in determination and creativity. He has seen people being mistreated and he's failed to act, but now, he will not fail to help wherever he can.

These days, David is authentically himself. Intelligent, but not arrogant or patronising. He is kind and embodies the values of an ally. There is never any judgement. Always support, guidance and a listening ear. David doesn't go into fix-it mode; he more curiously observes.

1: The central characters

Akua

Akua is passionate, well-connected and an ally across the board. She is driven to make changes in STEM. Akua has a motto she sticks to, "I believe more women should get involved in science, technology, engineering and mathematics (STEM) and be supported to take up leadership roles. I hope to play a part in seeing this vision realised within the next decade."

Dave

Dave is a natural ally with genuine empathy and understanding. He doesn't support women for the kudos points, but because he sees that the business world is still dominated by men who are often misogynistic. Dave wants to help women find their voice and, where he can, make sure they have a seat at the table. At all tables.

Farah

In true ADHD fashion, Farah thrives on variety. Security might be her mainstay, but her background is a tapestry of different roles: from marketing to being an artist and graphic designer to being deeply involved in campaigning and education.

Farah dedicates time to educating youth through Catcalls of London on social media and via workshops about consent, sexual harassment and community.

Farah's journey hasn't been straightforward. After returning from Africa, fitting into the typical corporate mould was a challenge, further complicated by undiagnosed ADHD, CPTSD and a brush with a cancer scare.

1: The central characters

Georgie

Mother, partner, leader and ambassador for herself and all women in technology. Georgina is Georgie to those who know her; she is as much a product of her environment growing up as she is a trailblazer for all women in technology. Honesty and humbleness are her superpowers, with tackling idiotic male leaders a focus of her efforts to redress the balance for all women in tech.

Georgie has forged a path that sees her leading teams, public speaking and writing about her specialism of IT – a male-dominated world that she is shaking up.

Ima

Ima is an experienced global communications professional with a successful PR, strategy and media relations track record.

She has been a transsexual all her life. Nothing to be 'proud' about; it's just how it is. From her early childhood, her parents were puzzled thinking that her being a girl was a phase that would pass, though strangers less so, but her girlish appearance let her get away with pretending to be a girl without too much trying. There were times when Ima would embrace this and play along, there were others when she hated being perceived as a girl but accepted that it was how things were.

Ima has experienced bullying, harassment and more negativity than most, but she remains committed to upholding LGBTQ+ rights and smiling while she does so.

1: The central characters

Lyra

Lyra is naturally funny, flirtatious and her behaviour can be a little outrageous. She is a hard worker and is desperate to land the next thing, then the next, then the next. Lyra experiences sexual harassment, sexual assault and bullying throughout her career. Lyra often thought that because of her character that she was to blame. After a while, Lyra was pushed to a point where she left her high-paying career to find safety and a slower pace of life.

Matthew

An IT operations leader, Matthew has considerable experience of working in a heterosexual world.

Matthew is homosexual and proud. However, questions like "How's your girlfriend?" and male homophobic behaviour are the bane of his life.

Russell

A good-looking, charming and clever chap. Always dressed in crisp suits or branded smart-casual attire and smelling of Jean Paul Gaultier – Le Male. Russell likes to support women in the workplace, especially those who have potential. But is Russell the ally we all think that he is?

Behind a good-looking, charming exterior, Russell is a sex pest who has a high opinion of himself. He can't hold a romantic relationship down because of his wandering eye. He appears to be very good at his job in professional services.

Saira

Saira started her career in law and soon realised that it wasn't quite for her. Since her pivot, Saira has taken the tech world by storm, launching multiple businesses and being a voice in different communities.

Samantha

"If your wardrobe isn't making you money, it isn't doing its job." This is one of the rules that Samantha lives by. She confidently clashes her outfits and is passionate about helping other women own the room. She wasn't always as confident as she is now. Samantha has experienced sexism, stereotyping and misogynistic behaviour, which she uses to fuel her drive for change.

Scott

Introverted Scott is the silent ally. He has been working for the same fashion house for longer than he likes to admit. Scott is a private man; he only shares his story and secrets with those he can trust. But those who are lucky enough to be friends with him know what an inspirational man he is. He is kind and filled with love and support for those around him.

Sophie

Sophie is the embodiment of integrity. It's this integrity that has seen others label her a soft touch – but she is anything but. Sophie is a woman who forges her own path, both in her career and life, whether forming her own consulting company, public speaking or aerial hooping in her spare time. Sophie is as formidable as she is fair.

Stephanie

Charming, sophisticated and well-travelled, Stephanie is still overwhelmingly hampered by self-doubt. Never more so than when working in the male-dominated Arab world.

Stephanie's speciality is acting as a builder of communities, bringing people together to solve life's complex problems.

Syed

Syed offers views that could be considered 'old school', sharing these views in scenarios and moments when they may not be wanted. He is a perfect candidate to learn more about allyship and instigate positive change.

If you are reading this and think it's about you, it probably is.

And if you troll us, you'll probably be in the next book.

CHAPTER 2: THE START OF IT

Lucy

In the trendy city of Bristol, Lucy embarked on her journey into the world of IT via a computing degree at the University of the West of England. With a passion for fashion and a bright, patterned scarf always wrapped around her neck, Paris chic she called it. She stood out in the sea of hoodies and casual attire.

As she entered the lecture halls filled with eager faces, Lucy never really noticed that she was one of the few women pursuing a degree in computing. Her focus was on getting to class on time (those £1 shots didn't help) and navigating the buildings (why were there so many?).

As the weeks went on, something made Lucy question her own choices. "What have I signed up to? This is so much harder that A level ICT," she thought. This was the start of imposter syndrome for Lucy, though at the time, this wasn't a term in her vocabulary.

She found herself in a ratio of around five women to more than 100 men. This didn't deter her, for she was driven by her own determination and knew that a career in tech would future-proof her.

If she did say so herself, Lucy's outfits were like artwork, carefully curated to show that she had other interests and passions outside of computing. Even her classmates commented on her unique sense of style, and she was once referred to as intimidating. Lucy laughed at the thought – that she, a 5ft4 brunette could be intimidating, and indeed, her classmates rarely approached her.

The journey through her computing degree was not without its challenges. There were times when the complex concepts left her feeling overwhelmed and frustrated. Doubts crept in, and she briefly considered quitting.

OK, maybe not briefly. It was at least once a week. But Lucy tried to be resilient. She persisted through the late nights, which she hated, the debugging struggles, where a third-year student did her coursework because Lucy knew how to work to her strengths. But there were more and more moments of self-doubt.

In between her second and third year, Lucy decided to take a break from her studies. Or, to be more precise, she officially quit! But was smart enough to defer the third year, just in case she changed her mind.

Lucy moved back home with her parents, who told her that if she wasn't going to be at university studying then she would have to get a job.

Within a few weeks, Lucy had lined up a number of interviews and ventured into the world of retail, starting her first official full-time job working at the local Boots on the high street. Lucy's natural conscientiousness meant she soon become a key-holder, where she had the privilege of opening and closing the store, as well as getting involved with regional store matters. Boots gave her the break from studies that she had needed, and the store manager, Sally understood this. One day over lunch, Sally broached the subject of university with Lucy.

"It's been a year, Lucy. As much as we love you being here and you could have a career in management with us, I think you should finish your degree. I never went to university and I regret it."

2: The start of IT

Sally wasn't that much older than Lucy. Having worked really hard in Boots after starting as a 'Saturday girl', Sally was a store manager at the age of 23, on a trajectory to becoming regional manager. She liked Lucy a lot as she reminded her of herself, but Sally had a concern that Lucy would regret not completing her degree. Lucy already had a student loan, too.

In her year working at Boots, Lucy gained more life experience then she could have imagined. Yet, it was during this time that she realised her degree in computing had given her more than just technical knowledge; it had equipped her with problem-solving skills and the ability to adapt in different environments. She knew if she wanted to go far, she needed to finish the fucking course.

Lucy returned to university. With renewed determination, she tackled her studies head-on. She made it work for her. While she still didn't find the subject matter as enjoyable as other endeavours, Lucy knew that this was the path that would lead to better things.

And so, after hard work and perseverance, Lucy graduated with her computing degree. She was even one of the first in her year to land a job.

And so her IT career began…

David

David's career began when he secured his first full-time job as a 16-year-old after leaving school with few qualifications, and he had zero intention of earning any. It wasn't that he was lacking in intelligence, he just couldn't see the importance of school work when socialising was so freely available.

2: The start of IT

David lived in a small industrial town in the UK, the sort you'd see on a BBC docuseries or crime drama. Not impoverished, far from it, but working class none the less. Upon leaving school, David realised that his location offered few choices – just the factories, the armed forces, college (no thanks) or joining a local job seekers' club. As a member of this club, David attended a practice interview as part of the job scheme, and it was here that he was asked the question, "Can you build a PC?" David's response was "Yes".

He didn't expect the interviewer to reply "Go and build one in that room."

In truth, David did have an affinity for technology as a youngster. He'd figured out how to make all of the school computers in his class play Axel F (from a CD in a magazine he'd bought), and he had done some related work experience. Outside of school, he had dabbled in the rubber keyboards of a Spectrum PC, played Elite and Horace Goes Skiing and become adept at spinning a 10p to get a 50p game at the arcades.

On this day, David built quite a few PCs. He'd seen some Microsoft DOS and Windows 3.11 installation discs in the room, so he set about installing these on every PC. David had quite the production line going when he saw a head pop round the door an hour later. They had expected him to be struggling when he'd been having a great time. He only made one small error, which was not wearing anything for anti-static, though luckily for him, no damage was done because of it.

With that, David was offered his first full-time job and started weeks before receiving his GCSE results. David's starting salary was £40 per week, which was approximately £9 less than his numerous newspaper and magazine delivery rounds. He kept all of these jobs for as long as he could, saving up for his first motorcycle at twice the speed he'd planned for.

David was over the moon. Within four weeks of leaving school, he'd stumbled into the next 30 years of his life, not that he knew it. It was never planned, and it certainly wasn't an ambition fulfilled.

Work was merely a tool to fund his 'life;' work certainly wasn't his life; David's life was going out, enjoying himself with friends and looking after only himself. That would change over time, as this Northern boy would migrate South to the bright lights and golden-paved streets of 'that' London.

"Individuals working in the private sector tend to switch occupations more often than those employed in public service."[1]

---

[1] *https://www.enterpriseappstoday.com/stats/career-change-statistics.html.*

CHAPTER 3: THE FIRST JOB

Lucy

"Your bum looks great in those trousers."

Inexperienced and naïve, Lucy turned to her manager and giggled, "Stop it, do you think?"

This wasn't the first time her line manager or the men in her team had made comments on her appearance. And it wouldn't be the last.

No one ever prepares you for leaving university. Or education, for that matter.

It must have been at least two weeks into the role, and Lucy questioned what she was doing there. Before this, she had only ever worked in a shop. On a shop floor, or in the shop manager's cupboard-style office.

Never in an 'office-office'.

She didn't know what the etiquette was. No one really told her. And did she feel safe? As in, physically safe? Everyone was talking to her as if she knew the acronyms of the thing that until five minutes ago wasn't even a thing.

If you don't join a graduate scheme, you find yourself out there on your own. The company Lucy joined didn't offer much mentoring or support, but luckily she met other 'younger' women, who gave her guidance and advice during her first few months.

"You can't really say those things, Lucy," one warned her when she complained loudly about an aspect of the job.

3: The first job

Lucy feared she would never get the hang of it.

As part of her role, Lucy was given access to material she never thought she would see at work. One of her daily jobs was to clear out blocked messages coming in and out of the company. To her horror, she discovered emails revealing workplace affairs and lad-like messages filled with swearwords and shocking objectification of women. Did these folks really know that IT monitored their inboxes and caught key words like 'F's and 'C's?

The final straw for Lucy was when a loan laptop came back to the office. Her activity was to clear any relevant search history and remove any data/files to ensure the laptop remained clean. Her manager looked over her shoulder to see that CTRL H had brought back pages and pages of porn.

"Don't click on that!" he panicked. "Give me the laptop and go and wash your hands," he ordered. "And on your way back, make us tea, love, we're a bit dry here."

Lucy didn't understand why she had been sent to make tea, until her colleague pointed out that those sites were not work-related and it was best she absent herself for a while.

The boss, for his quirks, wasn't happy about what they had found. Within the hour, he had spoken to the person who borrowed the laptop and advised that as per company policy, porn wasn't allowed on company devices.

This situation spurred a number of conversations where Lucy's male colleagues explained that this wasn't the first time it had happened. They told her about the guy in the basement office who watched hardcore porn on his big screen during the day. The lads seemed to enjoy telling Lucy and seeing the horror on her face. Were they getting 'kicks' out it?

Lucy hated this. She wanted out. She didn't want to work in IT anymore and she didn't want to work there.

David

David sat at his desk, headset on, fielding calls and resolving IT issues with practised ease. But it wasn't the technical difficulties of his customers that threw him off balance – it was Amanda, his manager.

Amanda was sharply dressed and incredibly confident; for a young man like David, she was as scary as she was attractive, her confidence oozed in every interaction. Every time she sauntered over to his desk to discuss a work task or review his performance, David couldn't help but feel a flutter in his stomach.

"Great job on that last incident, David," she'd say, her eyes locking onto his as she leaned just a little too close over his desk, her blouse catching David's eye as he fought with himself to look away.

"Uh, thank you, Amanda," he'd mumble, feeling both flattered and uncomfortable. Was she flirting? David was never quite sure; he was young and inexperienced in such matters. All he wanted was for the phone to ring again so he could get back to managing an incident, something he was much more comfortable with.

The confusion reached a tipping point at the company's summer social event. With the open bar and dimmed lights, it felt more like a private party than a work function. David tried to stick close to his younger colleagues, avoiding any awkward encounters with Amanda. But their paths inevitably crossed.

"Dance with me, David," Amanda said, her voice tinged with a suggestive note as she reached for his hand.

David hesitated, his mind racing. Firstly, 'Everything I Do' by Bryan Adams was not his scene and this was a line he was unsure about crossing. Politely but firmly, he declined. "I think I'd better not, Amanda. I don't want to mix personal and professional."

Amanda shot him a look – a mix of surprise and something he couldn't quite decipher – before shrugging. "Your loss," she said, turning to join another group.

The next week, David learned that Amanda was romantically involved with Mike, the colleague who sat just across from him. The revelation shook him; it added a layer of complexity to Amanda's advances that he hadn't considered. Was he a pawn in some office power play? Or simply a flirtation to pass the time? Either way, he realised how fraught the situation could have become had he agreed to that dance.

Looking back, David felt a mix of relief and concern. He was relieved he'd dodged a messy situation, but troubled by the notion that Amanda's advances might not have been as innocent as they seemed. Was it an abuse of power? Arguably so. Her position as his manager put him in a vulnerable spot, forcing him to weigh the implications of each interaction.

As the days passed, David began to distance himself, keeping their conversations strictly professional. He couldn't control Amanda's actions, but he could set boundaries to safeguard his own integrity.

David couldn't shake the feeling that he needed a change of scenery. He loved Manchester, the city he'd called home for years, but the challenge of the daily commute from his family home to Manchester and working in an office filled with complicated dynamics was taking its toll.

And then, like a sign from the universe, the perfect opportunity appeared: a new role in London. It was a significant step up, both in responsibility and pay. David was apprehensive; London was a big, bustling city far from his comfort zone. Yet, the idea was also exciting, and he decided to take the plunge.

The move to London was a whirlwind. The pace was faster, the stakes were higher, and the city was an ever-changing tapestry of people, places and experiences. David threw himself into work, relishing the challenges and opportunities that came with his new role. The absence of Amanda-like ambiguity was refreshing, too; it was a clean slate, a chance to redefine himself.

But London offered more than just professional growth. It also led him to Emma. Some of his friends met Emma during a holiday in Crete. The stars aligned when they decided to introduce the two of them at a local pub back in Surrey. It was the kind of warm, laughter-filled evening where everything seemed to click, and even though they began as 'just friends', they both knew something special was happening.

And just like that, the connection was made. Their first few 'friend' dates quickly turned into a deep, meaningful relationship, sealed after Emma broke her wrist and David spent eight hours with her in A&E.

Five years later, they were married. The years flew by in a happy blur of love, companionship and mutual growth.

Fast-forward to their 21st wedding anniversary, David looked at Emma and realised how much they'd been through together. Career moves, family tragedies and personal triumphs – through it all, Emma had been by his side, their love the one constant in an ever-changing world.

As he reflected on his journey from Manchester to London, from a young, confused helpdesk analyst to a seasoned professional, he realised how every choice he'd made had shaped the man he was today. The decision to move to London, the courage to step out of his comfort zone, the integrity to stand by his principles – they all led him to a life richer than he'd ever imagined.

Several years after leaving Manchester, David found himself back in town for a conference. While he was in a nostalgic mood, meeting up with old friends and colleagues, he couldn't avoid the inevitable gossip that had shaped the very office where he used to work. Over a pint at a local pub, an old mate pulled him aside.

"Dave, you wouldn't believe what's happened since you left. Do you remember Amanda and Mike?"

David felt a pinch in his stomach. "Of course, how could I forget?"

"Well, you know how everyone used to say there was something going on between them?"

David nodded.

His friend leaned in closer, almost whispering. "Someone apparently caught them on the CCTV, outside the office, late at night. Pants around ankles, on the car bonnet, the whole lot!"

David felt a mixture of shock, amusement and relief. "You're kidding!"

"Dead serious. The whole office has been talking about it for weeks, its mad that it was recently discovered, it was sent to us all via a burner email. It's like something out of a drama series."

David couldn't help but marvel at how he'd dodged a bullet by not getting entangled in whatever web Amanda had been weaving. He thought about his own journey since leaving Manchester, the growth in his career, and, most importantly, meeting Emma.

As he left the pub that night, David felt a renewed sense of relief. The rumours about Amanda and Mike served as a reminder of the dynamics and near-miss situations that could have steered his life in a very different direction. This wasn't a case of 'what-if', more of thanks that he'd made some decent choices.

It made him appreciate the life he'd built with Emma even more. The balance of love, trust and respect that they had couldn't be compared to any fleeting thrill – or potential disaster – that might have unfolded years ago on a car bonnet in Manchester.

He got into his taxi and smiled as it drove him back to his hotel. Some rumours are more than just idle talk; they can also serve as unexpected markers of how far you've come. And for David, that journey had been well worth it.

A study by Hewlett Packard found that:

"Men apply for a job when they meet only 60% of the qualifications, but women apply only if they meet 100% of them." [2]

---

[2] *https://hbr.org/2014/08/why-women-dont-apply-for-jobs-unless-theyre-100-qualified*. For more discussions surrounding this statistic, visit: *https://www.meridianbs.co.uk/resources/blog/should-i-apply-for-a-job-if-i-don-t-meet-all-the-requirements-/*.

CHAPTER 4: THE JOB DESCRIPTION

Lucy

Lucy's long lashes blinked with frustration as she read the job ad on her small iPhone 5c screen, *'The Service Delivery Manager is responsible for all aspects of IT, he will…'*

"*He!*" Lucy protested out loud, on the circle line. Her cheeks flushed with embarrassment. As her body temperature went up with anger, she felt herself go even pinker. Although, it could have been the tube carriage. Lucy tugged at her scarf and huffed as she tried to cool down. Looking back at her screen, did her eyes deceive her? No, Lucy really just read '*HE*'.

"The 1970s called; they want their sexism back!" Lucy mumbled, out loud again. She got an awkward glance from the girl next to her.

"Sorry," Lucy mouthed, and the girl looked away.

Lucy looked up, and realised the next stop was hers – St Paul's. She scrambled for her bag in her usual methodical order – phone away, Oyster card out and a double check to make sure she hadn't left or dropped anything. Lucy, originally from the seaside, had developed something of a London commuter march, which today could be described as full battle mode. She hiked up the escalator, taking two steps at a the time, cheeks flushed and an impatient look crossing her face as she queued to tap out of the station. With a pacey, puffy stride, she was taking no prisoners, accidentally knocking a 'suit' out of the way. She wanted to get to her desk, fast, so she could do something about that shocking job spec.

With her coat still on and beads of sweat glistening on her forehead, Lucy logged on to her thin-client. As it was finding a server to connect to, Lucy's frustration was bubbling further. She finally got into her machine and onto the jobsite where she had seen the ad. She was looking for a button or an email to report it but there was no way to contact them.

It was as if a lightbulb went off in her entire body... She started to furiously type into her browser "T-W-I-T-T-E-R-.-C-O-M".

Luckily for her, being in her position on the service desk, nothing was blocked.

Twitter loaded and she sent a tweet.

"*@ company in question: what's with the sexist job post?*"

She didn't really use Twitter, but thought what the heck anyway. She wasn't going to apply for the job, so nothing to lose, right? Even if it didn't have 'he', she couldn't apply anyway, she told herself. She did not have the experience or the qualifications stated. However, the benefits all aligned with Lucy's career goals, and some of the required skills, she did kind of have.

There was no way Lucy was going to apply for a job where she didn't meet at least 110% of the requirements. No way. She wasn't going to be caught out like that.

But as Lucy hit send on her tweet, she felt a surge of adrenaline. The small act of defiance made her heart race with excitement. She watched as the tweet garnered attention, with likes and retweets piling up within minutes. People were agreeing with her, echoing her sentiments about the outdated job description.

Feeling empowered, Lucy decided to take things a step further. She drafted an email to the company's HR department, just guessing the email. She outlined her concerns about the job posting and suggested changes to make it more inclusive. With a deep breath, she hit send and leaned back in her chair, feeling a sense of satisfaction wash over her.

As the day went on, Lucy received responses from both her tweet and the email. Her tummy turned, with an 'oh no, what have I done' and a 'hell yes, they should be emailing'. The company apologised for the oversight and promised to revise the job description to be more gender-neutral. They even asked for Lucy's input on how to attract a more diverse pool of candidates.

Because of her inexperience and fear, she didn't reply.

David

Years earlier, David was at his desk, staring at the computer screen, coffee in hand, pen in mouth, his BlackBerry buzzing away like an irritating wasp. He popped his coffee on the table mat. "Hmm, dirty mat," he thought to himself.

As David studied the job description on his ThinkPad, something caught his attention – the consistent use of 'he' throughout the document. David frowned, his interest in the opportunity slightly dampened by this detail. Why 'he', if this company were an equal opportunities employer? David had been in the workplace for ten years and remained stunned that even now in the 00's he was seeing and hearing 'he' everywhere.

David hadn't always thought this way. In fact, this was really the first time he'd noticed what he'd later come to understand as a pronoun. In this case, David noticed the gender bias because he'd reached a point in his career where he was writing job descriptions himself, and it seemed painfully obvious that you wouldn't want to exclude half the potential candidates by prefixing everything with the word 'he'.

"Surely everyone else gets that, too?" he pondered.

The job description was for a service delivery manager role at a reputable company. The responsibilities, qualifications and benefits all aligned with David's career goals and skills. However, the continuous use of 'he' in the text made him question whether the company held what he felt were outdated views on gender roles, and therefore whether they aligned with him at all.

He leaned back in his chair, considering his options. A part of him wanted to dismiss it as a minor detail and focus solely on the content of the job description. But his commitment to himself and to his own 'values' made him want to explore this further.

Ultimately, would it really impact him? Obviously not, in fact he was perfect for the job, not least because he was a 'he'.

David decided to seek counsel from his mentor, Paul. Paul wasn't exactly a passionate advocate for gender equality but he was a sensible chap and someone David could trust, especially with something as sensitive as looking for a new job.

Over lunch, David broached the topic cautiously. "Paul, I came across a job description that uses 'he' throughout. Do you think that's a bad thing? Is it worth challenging?"

Paul took a moment to munch on his Banh Mi before responding. "It's definitely worth a conversation, David. The language used in a job description often reflects the company's values and awareness of diversity, not to mention their attention to detail. While it might not have been intentional, the issue is worth addressing with them and raising awareness."

Later that day David drafted an email to the company's HR department.

In his email, he expressed his interest in the position and politely pointed out the repeated use of 'he' in the job description. He suggested to them the importance of gender-neutral language to ensure inclusivity for all potential candidates. He hoped his message would be received as a constructive suggestion rather than a criticism.

To his surprise, he received a prompt response from the HR manager, named Michelle. She thanked him for bringing it to their attention and assured him that the company was committed to inclusivity. Michelle explained that the use of 'he' was an oversight, not reflective of their values. She also mentioned that they were in the process of reviewing all their job descriptions to ensure they were gender-neutral.

David was pleasantly surprised by the response. He felt his concerns were heard but he wondered whether the company genuinely cared about delivering an inclusive environment.

Weirdly, he was now feeling less confident about the company's commitment, but being a male, he went ahead and decided to apply for the position. Maybe he could change things from within. As he worked on tailoring his CV and cover letter, he realised that his decision to address the issue had only reinforced his questions about the organisation and its real values.

A few weeks later, David received an email inviting him for an interview. The fact that weeks had passed concerned him. He overthought it and wondered if maybe they had received a high number of applications and needed time to sift through them all, or possibly they had spent that time reviewing other open roles, or they were just slow. Either way, the overriding feeling was one of concern.

During the interview, David had the opportunity to meet the hiring manager, Lisa, who explained the company's dedication to creating an inclusive workplace. Lisa shared their efforts in promoting diversity, not only in their hiring practices but also in their organisational culture.

David asked Lisa why they used 'he' repeatedly throughout the job description. Lisa looked shocked, startled even.

"I, I, I hadn't noticed. In fact, it is me who wrote that job description – well, at least the main responsibilities. When we finish the interview, I'll go to speak with HR as it's a surprise to me."

David felt bad; this wasn't Lisa's fault, but he also felt good that he'd raised the topic.

David left the interview feeling negative about the company's values and vision. He disliked their approach to addressing the language issue. Michelle had assured him that it was being addressed, yet Lisa looked shocked.

David didn't expect a job offer. He didn't receive one, and that company can be seen still using 'he' to this day.

"Having made these *[job]* applications, *the conversion to interview was 12% higher for women: in short, their applications were better. Women are also an astounding 24% more likely to be offered a job after having been interviewed."*
"The end result: after having made an application, women are 36% more likely to land the job than men. In essence, men are competing more but winning less."[3]

---

[3] *https://www.movemeon.com/insight/why-women-dont-apply-to-jobs*.

CHAPTER 5: THE INTERVIEWS

David

A few months later, David found himself preparing for a second interview with a company in the City of London, and he had some decisions to make. A pink shirt or a white shirt, cufflinks or buttoned cuffs? A navy suit and waistcoat were a given, a red tie for Liverpool FC a given too.

As he sat opposite John looking out over the River Thames, David noted John's cufflinks and decided he'd made the right choice of attire, though his cufflinks looked half as expensive as John's. David also spotted John's TAG Heuer watch and realised it made his Casio look a little cheap!

On the plus side, John could be David's future boss, and if he could afford a TAG and an Armani suit (spotted as he took his jacket off), then David would not be too far behind from a salary perspective.

The interview finished with a handshake and David was asked to wait for a few moments to discuss next steps. A lady named Nikki came in and pulled up a chair. As she sat down, David noted that her outfit was a little less 'professional' than he'd expected after seeing all the men in identikit suits and ties. She wore a lovely dress, with a high hem and a low-cut top. She seemed extremely stylish and confident, though David couldn't shake the feeling she was dressed for dinner and a club, not a post-interview checklist. He had no idea where to place his eyes, his mind racing as he concentrated firmly on The Tate Modern and the wonky bridge over Nikki's shoulder.

Nikki and David spent a few minutes discussing salary requirements and the benefits on offer. Nikki mentioned that David could join the team for a drink if he hung around until five, as Thursday was 'the new Friday', which felt a little uncomfortable to David, especially as earlier experiences had taught him to act with caution. Was she suggesting the two of them go for a drink? Surely not? In any case, it was best to make an excuse and retain professionalism.

It was 3 pm the next day when David pulled up to his in-laws' home in Surrey. He was just about to get out of his pride and joy, a BMW Mini Cooper, when the phone rang.

"Hi David, it's Nikki..." Nikki made some small talk, mentioning that David had missed a good evening and that one of the PAs was now the talk of the company – something to do with getting a little carried away after one too many Sambuca shots.

Nikki said that David had impressed throughout his interviews and that they'd like to offer him the job. He'd get the salary he was looking for, the benefits they'd promised and even his own view of St Paul's Cathedral from his office. On one condition...

"Could you cut your hair, or at least tie it up?"

David was shocked – a haircut? Why? What did his hair have to do with his ability to do a job? But then he snapped out of it as he remembered the £20k extra a year, potential five-figure bonus and those benefits.

"Sure, will a short back and sides do"? he asked.

"Haha!" said Nikki. "That sounds perfect. And don't worry, it's just our way. Welcome to the family! Expect the official offer letter next week. Have a good weekend."

David put the phone down and wondered just what he was getting himself into.

Lucy

Lucy waited nervously in reception. Each floor had a reception, an upgrade from where she was currently working. She looked around, and making sure no one was watching, she gave herself a little pinch – nope, this wasn't a dream. Lucy had always wanted to work for a bank; she had heard about the salaries, the benefits and the people. She had had no idea what to wear for this interview, so at the last minute she had panicked and bought a suit from Next, which was a little tight. As she had been working in a head office at a retailer, where jeans and T-shirts tended to be the 'uniform', she didn't have anything smart enough. Well, so she thought.

"Hi, Lucy." James, the head of the department, interrupted her thoughts. He was smiling and looked genuinely pleased to see her. This put her more at ease. She followed him into a meeting room surrounded by glass, like a fish bowl. She was centre stage for the IT department.

As she looked out, she could see mostly men, but there was a woman under a desk, she must have been doing some sort of desktop support. She looked over at her and gave her a polite smile.

The interview went well. Then another head of department came in and he clearly wasn't interested in asking competency-based questions.

"Do you play any sports?" he opened with.

Lucy froze. Her already uncomfortable suit-dress felt tighter. No, she did not play any sport. Her 'sports' were either running for the bus or spending the weekends shopping. She had a gym membership in the past. She wondered how the heck she was going to answer the question.

"I don't play any sport," she stammered, "but I do know that the bank sponsors the cricket and the rugby, and then there's the derby, right?"

The head of department smiled and ran his hand through his grey hair. His eyes widened, and Lucy started to wonder what was coming next. The voice in her head whispered, "You don't deserve to be here. They will find out you can't do this."

The next thing she knew, the normal four to five-stage interview was happening all at once. She was meeting the department. One bloke after another came in, looked her up and down, asked a random question, then exited.

In the brief second Lucy had to herself, she looked out onto the floor and saw the same brunette woman climb under another desk. She hoped that she wouldn't have to do the same if she was to be offered the job.

That woman was Georgie.

Georgie

Georgie had been working as part of a service desk team for a while. And this meant that at any given moment she might be required to lie under desks, reach up high to server racks or lug equipment around. Wanting to be seen as professional, she would wear trousers, appropriate-length dresses/skirts, shirts, jumpers and occasionally heeled shoes.

Georgie was thinking this as she looked back at the woman being interviewed, admiring her outfit.

Only the week before, when troubleshooting a monitor connectivity issue, she had to crawl under a user's desk in a skirt with heels, and a minute or so later, she felt something touch her ankle. The user she was assisting held her ankle and said he was being kind and helpful by removing a label from her shoe.

She felt deeply uncomfortable and vulnerable at that moment but totally powerless to share her concerns with anyone within the leadership team or HR, given the position held by the person she was supporting.

To protect herself, she vowed that she would never wear anything that could expose her in any way. Even though her male manager would often tell her that to be taken seriously and progress into a team leadership role she needed to dress the part, "be more feminine" and "wear dresses". When she did wear a dress, he was always the first to pass comment, often before she had even finished taking her coat off in the morning.

Georgie tried to catch Lucy's eye, to try to signal to her that this was not a supportive environment to work in, but it was too late – yet another member of the team had entered the room to interrogate her.

By 6 pm, Lucy's one-hour interview had lasted at least two hours, though thankfully the parade of men ceased, and she was escorted back to reception.

As soon as she got out of the building, Lucy scrambled for her phone to ring the recruiter. Upon his request, of course. This was Lucy to the T. She made sure she conformed. Being so early in her career, she was desperate to be liked. She was so desperate to climb the career ladder.

Of course, because of the time, the recruiter didn't answer. So she hopped on the tube and went about her evening.

The next day, the recruiter called.

"How did it go?" he said in his up-beat Australian accent.

Lucy put on her best 'posh', confident voice with a splash of self-doubt for good measure. She went into detail about her interview: who she met, what she was asked and how she handled it. She stopped now and again to do her practised awkward laugh. The recruiter laughed too and seemed surprised, wanting to know how Lucy had got to meet the other stakeholders. He promised to call her back and said she would probably get an offer by the close of play that day.

She did.

It was more money than she had expected and she obviously wasn't going to turn that down.

Lyra

Lyra shifted uncomfortably in the hard plastic chair provided in the nondescript meeting room, the kind that seemed designed more for quick, impersonal transactions than for comfortable, meaningful exchanges. The office, a temporary rental space in a faceless building in London's Shoreditch, carried a sterile air, punctuated only by the hum of an old heater struggling against the chill of a bleak January day.

As she adjusted her posture, trying to seem poised despite the discomfort, her interviewer's words startled her. "Do you have kids?" The question hung awkwardly in the cramped room. It was not what she had prepared for. It felt irrelevant, inappropriate, but there he was, looking at her expectantly, pen pursed between his lips.

5: The interviews

Lyra looked down briefly, noticing the dark splash marks on her shoes from puddles she'd hastily navigated earlier. She hoped they weren't too visible, a minor concern now amplified by her growing annoyance at that question. "Urm, no," she replied, trying to sound cute. "Don't you think I'm a bit young for that?" she said in a playful tone.

The man nodded, jotting something down before tossing another personal question into the mix. "So, are you married? Single? What's your deal?"

The informality of his tone, the casual intrusion into her private life, made Lyra's fidget in her seat. Throughout her academic career, she had been taught to expect questions about her skills or her experiences, but not her marital status or dating life. Yet, she felt like she had to comply, as if this man held all the cards to her future in London – a city where she hoped to start anew, escape the monotony of her current job, and truly begin her adult life.

She mustered a response, her voice a mix of resignation and flirtation. "I'm single, actually. Looking to move to London, like every 20-something after university, I guess." She giggled then tossed her hair back over her shoulder.

Lyra didn't even want this particular job. It was merely a stepping stone, a necessary leap towards her greater goal.

Yet, as the man scribbled more notes, she felt a sinking realisation that even unwanted opportunities had to be seized with a smile, maybe even to be a little flirtatious, especially when the alternative was staying stuck in a place she was desperate to leave. Somewhere she'd outgrown that no longer felt like home.

The questions continued, each a little more personal than the last, veering dangerously away from professional relevance.

Lyra continued to play it cool, giggling at the end of each answer, with a flutter of her eye lashes.

As the interview dragged on, Lyra's thoughts turned back to her university days, to the career advisor who had prepped her with mock interviews and CV tips. None had mentioned this scenario. There was no chapter in her textbooks on how to handle inappropriate questions, no lecture on the balance of power in an interview room.

She remembered that the career advisor had said that it was important to "be assertive, be confident, be prepared." But how could you prepare for this? The interview felt more like a first date! Finally, the interviewer set down his pen, offering a smile that didn't quite reach his eyes. "Well, Lyra, it's been really interesting. We'll be in touch." He winked as he stood up. Outside, the grey sky seemed to press down on the city. As she walked away, eager to distance herself from the weird experience, she made a silent promise to herself. If she was going to make it in London and navigate her adult and professional life she would need to be more than prepared; she would need to be resilient. She would use her personality to get where she wanted to go.

"Less than a third (32 per cent) of employers had enforced interview training for cultural understanding, sensitivity, and competence, while half (50 per cent) of those polled received no training on inclusive hiring before interviewing applicants."[4]

"The Slater and Gordon survey also revealed that 40% of managers avoid hiring younger women to get around maternity leave."[5]

---

[4] *https://www.peoplemanagement.co.uk/article/1805736/less-third-employers-mandated-interview-training-around-inclusivity-study-finds*.

[5] *https://culture-shift.co.uk/resources/workplace/maternity-discrimination-in-the-workplace/*.

CHAPTER 6: THE OTHER SIDE OF THE TABLE

David

David sat nervously in the meeting room, reviewing his notes for the upcoming interview. Making sure he thoroughly understood everything about the job description in front of him – the job description he'd written.

He was interviewing candidates for a senior position on his team, and one of them was Elizabeth, an accomplished professional with an impressive track record. David was determined to be fair and open-minded, ensuring he didn't let any biases cloud his judgement.

"Look her in the eye," David said to himself. "If you like what she's wearing, resist the urge to say so." As Elizabeth entered the room, David stood up and extended his hand. "Hello, Elizabeth. Thank you for coming. Please have a seat."

Elizabeth wore a formal trouser suit and a white blouse, her hair tied back in a bun. Nothing for David to feel uncomfortable about.

"Thank you, David," Elizabeth replied with a warm smile. She took a seat across from him.

David began by asking about Elizabeth's qualifications and experiences. He was impressed by her responses, but knew he had to word his questions carefully.

"So, Elizabeth," David said, "how do you manage your work-life balance?"

Elizabeth tilted her head thoughtfully. "Well, I believe in maintaining a healthy work-life integration. It's essential to find a balance that suits both my career goals and personal life. This comes from me making time for the things that are important to me. The best version of me is one that makes time to achieve my work and personal objectives. Last year it was to complete my MBA, this year it's training for a marathon. Some of my best ideas come when I'm running, ideas about work or otherwise."

David nodded, relieved at how he had phrased the question, rather than asking about 'managing family time'. He asked Elizabeth about her leadership style and problem-solving approaches.

As the conversation flowed, David found himself increasingly self-conscious. He noticed that he stumbled over his words whenever he tried to recognise Elizabeth's achievements. He wanted to do so without sounding condescending or sexist.

"I must say, Elizabeth," David said, "your accomplishments are really…impressive. I mean, your track record is quite remarkable."

Elizabeth chuckled softly. "Thank you, David. I appreciate that."

The interview continued, and David's uneasiness grew. He realised he was overthinking every word he spoke, trying not to make a blunder. He wanted to ensure he treated Elizabeth with the same professionalism he would extend to any candidate, regardless of gender, race or religion. He found it a delicate balancing act.

At one point, David tried to steer the conversation towards diversity and inclusion, wanting to emphasise the importance of an inclusive workplace. He cleared his throat nervously. "So, Elizabeth, diversity is something our company values greatly. How do you see yourself contributing to our diverse team?"

Elizabeth nodded, seemingly unfazed by his question. "Diversity is crucial for creativity and innovation. I believe in creating an environment where everyone's unique perspectives are valued and encouraged."

As the interview drew to a close, David felt a mix of relief and frustration. He knew he had been overly cautious, second-guessing his every word to avoid any hint of sexism. At the same time, he realised that his intentions were genuine, and he wanted to be fair and unbiased.

"Thank you, Elizabeth," he said. "It was a pleasure speaking with you today."

"The pleasure was mine, David," Elizabeth replied, standing up. "I appreciate the opportunity to discuss the role."

As Elizabeth left the room, David let out a sigh. He had realised that equality was about treating everyone individually, acknowledging their talents and experiences, and avoiding unnecessary apprehensions. As he prepared to interview the next candidate, he hoped to find a balance between being respectful and avoiding undue self-consciousness.

David also reflected on something else: Why on earth was his company not providing training and support for the interviewing and hiring process? Should he raise this at the next leadership meeting?

Lucy

"Now, that's what I call a fantastic interview!" beamed Lucy to her director, Derek.

"Do you think we would look a bit desperate if we issued her the offer this evening?" Derek said in his usual cautious tone.

Lucy paused for a moment. Should she say it? Her values were conflicted; after rounds and rounds of terrible interviews, this had probably been one of the best interviews she had ever conducted.

"Derek," Lucy began. "There's just one concern."

"What is it?"

Lucy took a deep breath, and then another. "Do you think she will just join, pass her probation then go off and have kids? She is about to get married, which is great. But what about if she then goes and has a baby? We would be back to square one again."

Derek paused. He knew Lucy well and knew she was just trying to protect the team. He shared the sentiment that interviewing for this role had been a bit of a disaster. But as a father of two, he had a different opinion.

"I don't think that is a concern we need to worry ourselves with. I think we need her as much as she needs us. And life happens."

Lucy immediately felt guilty for what she had said. She apologised and swiftly changed the flow of conversation. "So, shall I go back to HR to issue her an offer letter?"

"In recent years, an increasing number of tech companies have stepped up their efforts in hiring diverse talent, with diversity, equity, and inclusion (DEI) a significant priority. However, women continue to be under-presented in the male-dominated tech sector."

"Globally, women make up only 28% of the technology workforce. In the EU, women make up less than 20% of IT workers in the sector, only occupying 22% of all tech roles across European companies."

"In China it is a slightly more optimistic picture. Based on a survey by Silicon Valley Bank, 70% of tech start-up firms have one or more females in Chief Executive Officer roles. However, according to data published by Boss Zhipin, the largest online recruitment platform in China, women still only make up less than 20% of the most popular tech positions."[6]

---

[6] *https://www.gravitasgroup.com/blog/gender-equality-in-tech-the-causes-of-under-represented-women-in-tech#.*

CHAPTER 7: THE BIRD IN IT

Georgie

Georgie sat in her small home office, she could hear birds singing cheerfully outside the window. She had just finished her first cup of coffee and was reflecting on her 18-year journey in the IT industry. The highs and lows of Georgie's career played out like scenes from a novel in her mind, each moment appearing in vivid clarity. The highs were harder to recount without referring to her CV, but the lows came flooding back.

Georgie's journey had started with various service desk roles, where she steadily climbed the ranks within service desk and infrastructure teams. Her interviews had been a mixed bag of excitement and frustration. Questions like "Do you mind being the only girl?" and statements such as "You will be the youngest in the team/company" were common. At the time, she had accepted these comments as the norm. In college, she had been one of three females in a class of 30, and by the final year, she was the only female to successfully complete the course. University was even more imbalanced, with Georgie being one of three women among approximately 90 IT degree students.

Fitting in seemed like the only option. She became one of "the lads", a fan of sports, a follower of football, and naturally gravitated towards male friends. It was a survival mechanism in a world that seemed designed to exclude her.

As the years passed, Georgie became known as 'the bird in IT'. Banter was rampant, and social gatherings often felt like a target game, with her as the target. Conversations with men outside of her close colleagues were always subject to speculation about romance despite her interactions being strictly platonic.

In the early to mid-00's, addressing such a culture was not the done thing.[7] If brought up, the accuser was often seen as a troublemaker. News articles of that era echoed similar narratives, where women raising discrimination cases often walked away jobless. Georgie didn't address it, and neither did her colleagues. Today, she would turn to allies and start conversations, ensuring that such behaviour was called out and dealt with. But back then, she had to adapt and endure.

Carving her space in a service desk team was one challenge; doing the job and dealing with other people's pressure or microaggressions was another. Although colourful language was often toned down in her presence, the volume was not. She remembered a particularly aggressive user shouting at her across the office at 6:30 in the morning, demanding she fix his password. On another occasion, a user's repeated and increasingly loud criticisms reduced her to tears. Apologies, if they came, were often delayed and insincere.

Then came the comments about her appearance. "You are only successful in interviews because you are young and attractive" and "You were hired because they thought you were fit," were just a couple of the remarks that stuck with her, shaping how she presented herself at work and in her personal life. Dressing appropriately for a job that required both a professional appearance and physical activity was a constant challenge.

---

[7] *https://www.theguardian.com/society/2023/sep/25/for-too-long-women-have-been-bullied-and-demeaned-by-lad-culture*.

An incident that particularly stood out was when she had to crawl under a user's desk to fix a monitor connectivity issue. Feeling something touch her ankle, she was startled to find the user removing a label from her shoe. His claim of being helpful did nothing to alleviate her discomfort and feelings of vulnerability. Reporting such incidents seemed pointless given the power dynamics at play.

Navigating her career path, Georgie faced a critical choice between a technical specialist role or a service delivery team leadership role. She sought mentorship from a male leader who was keen to mould her into his protégé. However, their leadership styles clashed. Georgie's empathetic, personable approach was at odds with his business-focused, results-at-any-cost mentality. This was when she learned a crucial lesson: leadership must be authentic and aligned with one's values.

One of her first leadership roles was particularly eye-opening. She led a small team responsible for service delivery, and they formed close bonds. However, after confiding in a team member about feeling unwell due to "women's issues", she later discovered that her team had created a recurring calendar entry every 28 days about it. This breach of trust solidified her 'soldier on' approach, making work no longer feel like a safe space to admit vulnerability.

Despite these challenges, Georgie had forged a successful career, inspiring and promoting others along the way. She recalled a disheartening conversation while recruiting for a team, where a colleague expressed reluctance to hire a female due to the physical demands of the role. Georgie used herself as an example to challenge this stereotype, emphasising the importance of hiring based on ability rather than gender.

Working in a male-dominated industry, Georgie had made close friends among her male colleagues. Some were like family, offering support and encouragement. However, a comment from one such friend during a job hunt floored her: "In this DE&I era, surely you are a shoo-in to be the diversity hire anywhere." The remark made her question her achievements and the underlying motives behind her career advancements.

There was still a long way to go, despite the progress in diversity, equity and inclusion. Georgie often found herself defaulting to tasks like recording meeting minutes or writing on whiteboards in brainstorming sessions, provoking frustration and exhaustion. She was not the team's sweetheart or the friendly face of IT who would deliver bad news because people wouldn't shout at her. She was an advocate for change, determined to see that others didn't experience the same struggles.

Fortunate to have met and been inspired by incredible allies, Georgie's self-development journey involved investing in coaching, mentoring and networking. She discovered a community passionate about creating a safe and inclusive space for future generations in the service management industry. Reflecting on her career, Georgie felt a renewed commitment to challenging outdated behaviours and fostering an environment where everyone could thrive.

As she closed her eyes and took a deep breath that morning, Georgie knew that the path ahead was still fraught with challenges. But with each step, she was determined to make a difference, not just for herself, but for all those who would follow in her footsteps.

"The most common assumption people gave for why they were rejected [following job applications]: there were too many other applicants (43%). However, 35% of women thought they were rejected because they'd asked for too much money compared to 27.3% of men."[8]

[8] https://www.fastcompany.com/90763477/survey-how-many-rejections-job-seekers-lose-confidence-joblist.

CHAPTER 8: THE JOB OFFER/REJECTION

David

David had always been an early riser, a habit he maintained meticulously to allow for a brisk morning run or a walk with his dog before the city stirred. By 7 am, he was in his London office, settling down with a lovely Pret extra-strong mocha, sifting through the emails that had accumulated overnight. It was 2008, and the digital world was bustling, yet David made sure to carve out this time for himself before diving into his work day. Today, however, his routine was charged with an unusual sense of anticipation.

The-all-too familiar buzz of his BlackBerry signalled the arrival of a particularly awaited message as he unlocked his screen. There it was – an email from Nikki:

> **Subject:** David Barrow, Snr Service Delivery Manager – Job Offer

His heart thudded with a mix of excitement and apprehension as he tapped to open it.

"Bloody hell," he muttered under his breath as he scanned the contents. The offer was generous, featuring a salary and bonus structure that far exceeded his current compensation. It was the kind of leap that could drastically change his lifestyle and allow for more than just comfortable savings.

But as he delved deeper into the offer letter and accompanying documents, his initial excitement dampened.

The role itself, a senior service delivery manager, was what he had always aimed for – the culmination of years of hard work and dedication. However, a glaring issue leaped out at him from the pages. The job description, the contract, even the welcome letter, didn't ever refer to him as 'David' though it consistently used 'he'. No 'she', always just 'he'. It was as though the documents were crafted decades ago, untouched by the evolution of society.

David had never considered himself an activist. He wasn't one to attend rallies or shout about injustices from the rooftops, but he believed in equality. It irked him – more than that, it angered him – that such oversight still took place.

Sitting back, he felt a familiar frustration boil inside him. He wondered why it seemed so difficult for HR departments and hiring managers to step into the modern age.

He weighed his options. He could accept the job, pocket the significant raise and just deal with the outdated language. After all, what did he care, really? Sexism didn't affect him directly. He pondered over the kind of environment he'd be stepping into, one that possibly still harboured such archaic views. Would he be able to overlook these issues day in, day out?

In the end, the temptation of the generous salary and the prestige of the role won out over his initial reservations. He pressed 'send' on his acceptance email, feeling a mix of satisfaction and unease.

Ultimately, David thought, as he celebrated with a Katsu curry and pint that lunchtime, he and his wife needed the money – he didn't want to cut off his nose to spite his face.

However, the unease quickly grew in the following weeks. David started his new role, and the reality of the company's culture began to unfold. The gendered language in the job documents was not just an oversight but a reflection of a broader, more ingrained issue. He noticed a lack of diversity in leadership roles, subtle biases in meetings, and an overall culture that did not challenge outdated norms but, instead, quietly upheld them.

David found himself increasingly uncomfortable, realising that by accepting the position, he had compromised his values for financial gain. He witnessed instances where female colleagues were overlooked or subtly dismissed, their contributions not receiving the acknowledgment they deserved. The realisation that he was part of an organisation that perpetuated these disparities weighed heavily on him.

Weeks into the job, David sat at his new desk late one evening, the office quiet around him, reflecting on his decision as he looked out onto the city streets below. By now, he would usually be on the cobbled stone of Leadenhall Market supping a Guinness, but he was not feeling it tonight.

The money was good, yes, and on paper, his career had never looked better. Yet, he felt a profound sense of regret. He had chosen to ignore his principles when they had been tested, and now he was complicit in a system he knew was unfair.

The regret had culminated immediately before this chilly evening when, during a meeting, a particularly overt instance of sexism played out. One of his male colleagues interrupted a female project manager mid-presentation to "simplify what she was trying to say", even though she was clearly the expert in the room. David saw the resignation in her eyes, and it mirrored his own.

That night, David knew he had made a mistake. No job, regardless of the financial rewards, was worth sacrificing his core beliefs for. The decision to stay with the company became untenable. David began to plan his next steps, determined to align his career with his values, no matter the cost.

David left the office, ignoring the pub and feeling more determined but also more isolated than ever before. His usual commute home on the Thameslink train was at this time of night a time for him to unwind, listen to music or catch up on his latest magazine subscription, GQ.

However, tonight was different. His mind raced, replaying the events of the past months, the compromises he had made, and the cultural malaise he had witnessed. He was so lost in thought that he barely noticed the rowdy group at the end of the carriage, their laughter piercing his reverie.

As the train neared his stop, he stood and made his way to the door, trying to shake off the heaviness in his mind. Just as he stepped off, a sudden shout cut through the noise of the bustling station. "Yuppie c%$t!" The words stung, but before he could turn to face the speaker, a can of beer flew past him, splashing its contents over his Dior coat. The perpetrator, a visibly drunk man, jeered from the safety of the departing train.

Stunned and soaked in beer, David stood on the platform, the cold, yeasty smell enveloping him. The insult, though hurled by a stranger in a drunken stupor, felt oddly poignant, especially as it was a can of Guinness that covered him.

Had he really become the type of person he had always disliked? Was this working-class Northern lad now just another corporate drone, indistinguishable from the countless others, absorbed in a world of superficial success?

This unsavoury end to an already troubling day was a stark wake-up call. David realised that the dissonance between who he was and who he wanted to be had grown too great to ignore. He needed to make a change, not just for his career but for his sense of self. The world might see him a certain way, but he didn't have to accept that definition. He needed to find a path that aligned with his values, where he didn't just succeed financially but felt true to himself.

This moment of humiliation, oddly clarifying in its brutality, cemented his resolve. David decided then and there that he would seek his wife Emma's counsel, and with her approval would resign first thing in the morning. He would seek out opportunities where respect, integrity and fairness were not just platitudes but practices. Where being an ally wasn't an act of defiance, but a requirement.

As he walked home from the station, his steps grew lighter with each block. The night was still cold, and his coat still damp, but a fire had been lit within him. David was ready to start anew, this time on his own terms.

Lucy

"They really liked you," said the recruiter on the other end of the phone. Lucy's pulse quickened with anticipation of what was sounding like a positive outcome.

"But…" Oh, maybe not.

Lucy felt a lump in her throat.

"It was just that you talked too much about travelling with work, and it isn't something they can accommodate. They were worried that you would take the job, then in a few months quit for another role that would be international, or take a gap year – considering your age."

Lucy didn't know what to say. She had blown it. "Oh, that's a shame," she managed. "Was all the other feedback quite positive, then?"

The recruiter explained that it was indeed positive, and after politely ending the call, Lucy returned to her desk. She made a mental note to be more careful in how she represented herself in the future.

Lyra

Lyra got on well with people. She had a natural ability to find a connection with someone, ask lots of questions and help them open up.

She had applied for a job via a recruiter called Dean. He seemed nice enough. She could tell he had taken a shine to her and she was using this to her advantage. Lyra would giggle at Dean's jokes and talk about personal things. She 'let slip' she was single and how she was finding it hard to meet someone. Dean could relate.

Lyra knew what she was doing. But she was desperate for this new job and could do with the salary increase. Since leaving her job at the bank, she was missing the large bonuses and wasn't able to save as much money as she would have liked.

After another phone call one afternoon, Dean asked Lyra if she would like to meet in London for a drink if she got the job.

8: The job offer/rejection

"Yeah, sure, yeah – that would be cool," Lyra lied. She had seen his picture on LinkedIn and he most certainly wasn't her type, so she had no intention of going. If he had been hot, then maybe one drink wouldn't have hurt. She was single after all...

They ended the call. Within five minutes, Dean had texted her.

She opened the message. It read:

> **Maybe this will sweeten the deal x.**

And below the text was a photo of his penis.

"WHAT?!" she screamed.

For a minute, Lyra couldn't breathe. She was disgusted. But inside, she had an uneasy feeling that she had led Dean on, and prompted him to think it was OK to send such a picture.

How was she going to handle this? What on earth was she going to do?

She was at her family home at the time. She ran down the stairs to tell her parents about it – half laughing and half in shock. Lyra's parents were pretty open minded but were also taken aback.

"I think you had better tell him that this isn't acceptable, Lyra," her father advised. "And delete the photo from your phone."

Lyra sighed loudly and tapped into her phone:

> **Are you kidding me? This is highly unprofessional and I have in mind to report this to your line manager.**

Lyra still had a little bit of guilt. She knew she had flirted too much, but she equally knew she hadn't asked for this. This was sexual harassment, wasn't it?

Dean, clearly in a panic, apologised. And they never talked about it again.

Lyra got the job at the insurance firm. And Dean had the audacity to ask her out for drink, again. Lyra turned him down. She also blocked his number and his LinkedIn, and they never crossed paths again.

"More than 93% of employers believe that onboarding plays a critical role in an employee's decision to stay or leave the company."[9]

_____

[9] *https://www.think-learning.com/onboarding/onboarding-statistics/*.

CHAPTER 9: THE FIRST DAY

Lyra

Lyra woke up with a mix of excitement and nerves, ready to start at her new job. As a lover of fashion, it was important to her to choose the right outfit, so she picked out her favourite dress, which was green with a tiger motif, hoping it would give her a confidence boost. She made sure she arrived early, before the 8 am agreed time. Walking into the sleek office building, she felt a surge of anticipation. Today was the beginning of a new chapter.

Lyra's excitement quickly turned into anxiety, however, when she was greeted by an empty reception desk and no sign of the orientation team she was told would be there.

Lyra sat in the reception, scrolling through her emails to find a contact from the recruitment girl that sent her all the details.

She was just about to give up and go home, tears pricking, when a woman in a pink and red dress appeared, heels clicking as she rushed in and held out her hand.

"Hi there, you must be Lyra. I'm Lucy, one of the senior managers here," the woman said, with slightly laboured breath, her cheeks flushed. Registering the confusion on Lyra's face, Lucy added, "I'm terribly sorry I'm late the traffic this morning was a nightmare. And trying to drive in these new shoes, was an epic fail on my behalf." Relief washed over Lyra as she shakily introduced herself to this kind-faced and stylish woman.

"I'm so sorry again," Lucy continued. "There was a mix-up with the schedules today and the orientation team aren't available. But I am, so let's get you sorted out."

Lucy's presence was like a beacon of light. She gave Lyra a tour of the office, showed her to her desk, introduced her to her team members and guided her through the computer set-up process. Lyra began to feel more at ease, her earlier nervousness gradually dissipating.

Throughout the day, Lucy made sure Lyra felt included and supported. They ate lunch together, and Lucy introduced her to more of her colleagues. By the end of the day, Lyra no longer felt like a lost outsider but rather a welcomed member of the team.

She left the office with a lightness in her step, grateful for the unexpected ally and friend she'd found in Lucy on her very first day. With her work bag slung over her shoulder, Lyra decided to take a detour through the bustling streets of London instead of heading straight home.

The city was alive with people streaming out of office buildings, hurrying towards tube stations or queuing at bus stops. Lyra wove through the crowd, her senses tingling with the myriad sounds of the city: the distant wail of sirens, the conversations of commuters, and the occasional laughter spilling out from London's many pubs.

As she walked, the dense urban landscape opened up to reveal the sweeping River Thames. Lyra found herself drawn towards the water's edge, the earlier events of the day replaying in her mind. The feel of the cool breeze off the river was refreshing, and she paused to watch the sun begin its descent, casting an orange glow.

9: The first day

Leaning against the railing, Lyra allowed herself to truly absorb the enormity of her move to London. Today had been challenging, but it had also shown her that even in the vast anonymity of this city, connections could be made, support could be found. Lucy's kindness had not just helped her navigate the practicalities of a new job; it had also marked the start of what she hoped would be a significant professional relationship.

As she watched a river boat lazily drift past full of revellers, Lyra felt a surge of optimism about her future. Today *could* indeed be the first step towards building a career she could be proud of in a city that was full of opportunities. She felt a quiet confidence that she could not only survive but thrive here, and she was eager to see what her new life in London had in store for her and her tiger dress. As she melded back into the crowd, Lyra resolved to no longer be just another face in the crowd; she was a woman on the precipice of something truly great.

"It is estimated that around 90 per cent of sex workers are female. Although male stripping does exist in the UK, it often looks very different, with troupes like the Dreamboys performing on stage in front of large crowds. This summer [2024], for example, the Dreamboys will be performing at the Grand Opera House York and Swansea Grand Theatre. They even have a regular slot at a nightclub in Bristol, but because they do not perform fully nude they avoid the need for an SEV [sexual entertainment venue] licence. Unlike their female counterparts, they are not at risk of being closed down."[10]

---

[10] *https://www.prospectmagazine.co.uk/society/38722/the-naked-truth-about-strip-clubs*.

CHAPTER 10: IN DA CLUB

Lucy

"We're going to Browns," one of the team members said with a smile.

"OK, is that the one in Covent Garden?" Lucy asked.

"No, it's near King's Cross."

"I didn't know there was a Browns in King Cross," Lucy thought. She followed the team, and upon arriving, she realised this was a completely different type of venue to the Browns she knew.

Going to a strip club didn't trouble her as she was desperate to fit into the group. She found it odd that she had to walk through the 'private dancing' part to go to the toilet. But what was stranger was how two of her six male colleagues stayed by her side all night, paying for her drinks and popping a £1 in the pint.

"You don't have to babysit me," Lucy told them.

Her manager, looking uncomfortable, made a slightly slurred remark about how he wasn't having a good time and was happy to talk to her.

Lucy was the only female in the room who wasn't in their underwear. She wondered if this made the men feel uncomfortable. Or whether they even noticed. She didn't really care. She was actually quite enjoying herself, seeing what really went on inside these kinds of places.

Lucy caught an eye of a man she didn't know, who looked out of place. He smiled at her. She smiled back. She then gave him her sarcastic eye roll to indicate 'this place huh?!' and he grinned and turned away.

Lucy turned back to admire the women. They were all beautiful in their own way. Lucy wanted to support all women, whatever their job, including stripping.

Her thoughts were interrupted.

"And, she is only doing this to get through law school," Ben slurred. Lucy's teammate Ben was having a fun night. As a rugby player, he could handle his drink – but tonight Lucy thought he'd had a little too much.

"How are you getting home?" she asked. "It's quite late."

"Can I sleep on your sofa," Ben responded.

If it was anyone else, Lucy would have hesitated but Ben was kind and would never try anything with her, surely. In fact, he had said she was like a sister once.

Even in his drunken state, Ben paid for the cab back to Lucy's flat, which she shared with her friend. The next day, Ben bought them breakfast and coffee. He respected that Lucy was trying to fit in with the group and hoped she didn't feel too uncomfortable with it all.

That night wasn't spoken about again at work.

David

"Don't worry, I don't need a shit."

These were the words the woman said to David as she grabbed him, leaned over his shoulder and watched him go to the toilet. It's not unusual for the door to open when you are mid-flow; all men know that you head straight for the urinal, head down, and quietly do your best not to splash yourself or others.

But, to have someone grab you from behind and then lean over your shoulder is most unusual; for them to look down, check your appendage and whisper, *"Don't worry, I don't need a shit"* is even more unusual. Yet this is what happened to David as he did his business. It's hard to know how that made him feel at that very moment.

David was in a strip club called Browns, an environment where men usually felt they had the power, yet he certainly, felt powerless right now. He pretended to urinate before shuffling out hurriedly.

As he re-entered the room, he began to plot his escape. A professionally dressed young woman caught his eye. David was puzzled. She seemed happy enough to be there among all the men, but then she did an eye roll, which he interpreted as 'what is this place?' He smiled, then began to sidle to the back door.

Maybe this was an environment where women were more in control than he'd thought. Certainly, his toilet partner, with a pint glass full of coins in her hand, had held all the power moments before.

This type of socialisation was part of David's job; some thought it was fun and important, but it had felt at odds with David's values over the years. Age, experience, marriage and living in a diverse and inclusive city in Brighton had changed his views on the world and his role within it.

Brighton has also changed David's style. When offered the job, his employer had asked him to cut his long, rockstar hair. Now, several years later, he had used his three months' notice to grow a decent quiff. As it was a Friday, he had discarded his suit, thrown on his Armor Lux top, Gramicci pants and a nice pair of Clarks to finish the look.

That day, this day of powerlessness, marked David's second-to-last day as an IT manager for a worldwide marketing firm in the City of London, and it hadn't come soon enough. His leaving drinks resulted in him getting home on the last train at 1 am.

David's final day began as always with a bus at 5:09 am, followed by the 1 hour 30-minute train travel from Brighton to London Blackfriars. Of course, the train was delayed at Haywards Heath, allowing him to catch up on some sleep and to think. He recalled the evening that a drunk man had screamed 'Yuppie c%$t' as he threw a beer can at him; on his third day in the job.

Linking this to the woman who appeared over his shoulder, David felt that these two unconnected invasions of his privacy seemed to describe this period of his life.

That morning, David arrived at his desk at 06:55 am, second into the office. As always, Michael stirred as David's presence awoke him from under his desk.

David sat at his desk, looked out to St Paul's Cathedral, placed his extra strong Pret mocha on the coaster (he always used a coaster), unwrapped his breakfast bap and opened his laptop – ready to get to work here for the last time.

Over the next 90 minutes, familiar faces strolled into the office in various hungover states.

"Good night last night…a few too many, though." A common theme from Andy.

"Where did you get to?" asked Nathaniel.

"Home, mate," David replied. "Some of us need some sleep."

"Ha ha! Sleeping is for girls," Phillip responded. "Speaking of girls – let me guess where you all landed up…"

"Yep – Browns," Andy confirmed. "Pound-in-a-glass night – and maybe a good pounding after, hahaha!"

David smiled, but inside, he was squirming. That final night in Browns, that invasion of privacy and the feelings the evening had brought up would go on to have quite an impact on his working life.

As would the young professional woman who had appeared to be enjoying herself that night.

"75% of workers who voluntarily leave their jobs do so because of their bosses and not the position, the role itself or the company."[11]

"And a study in 2022 suggests the culture of quiet quitting is down to bad bosses."[12]

---

[11] *https://sewells.com/employees-dont-leave-companies-leave-managers/.*

[12] *https://hbr.org/2022/08/quiet-quitting-is-about-bad-bosses-not-bad-employees.*

CHAPTER 11: HORRIBLE BOSSES

Lucy

"You are just a southerner softy," said Amber.

"Such a shame," thought Lucy, "that this woman has to behave this way."

Still inexperienced, Lucy had finally got her opportunity to grow. She felt secure at the insurance firm – the people were nice; she knew the head of the Infosec from her first job and…the best time she had was when her line manager was off on bereavement. She wished she could feel guilty about it, but Amber was a nightmare to work for.

Amber was direct. She didn't mince her words. She did her due diligence. She was clever, technically adept and perhaps everything you could ever want in a head of IT support role – but goodness, she was a bit of a cow. She made grown men cry. Lucy had seen it.

Amber always looked good, too. She wore fashionable office clothing. She carried a notebook and a purple pen. Lucy suspected the purple pen was so no one else would steal it. And if she liked you, you were safe – but if she didn't – that was another story.

As much as she wanted to, Lucy didn't hate Amber. She quite liked her directness. There were elements to Amber's personality that Lucy wanted to copy.

She just wanted Amber to be a little nicer.

Lucy wasn't the only person who felt this – her colleague Dre would open up over their 8 am coffees when the office was quiet. Dre had been at the company for a while, had a great team and a great work schedule. The only issue was he hated working for Amber. She would constantly pull his work apart, tell him his team was rubbish and bully him into the ground.

Lucy and Dre made a plan to speak to HR. It wasn't that they wanted to get Amber into trouble, but they wanted it to be a less hostile environment.

The HR meeting was a waste of time. Like Dre, Amber had been in the business a long time and was good at her job. She blamed the miscommunication on a culture clash between the Scottish and English, claiming her English colleagues didn't understand her Scottish directness. And the rest of the meeting became somewhat of a blur to Lucy and Dre.

A few months later, the company had a huge restructure. The team Dre managed was moved up north, which meant his southern-based team and his role were made redundant. This also meant, Amber's role was reduced, which led her to leave the company herself. Karma, Lucy thought.

Lucy on the other hand, well her role was also at risk, but she had already started to network with the new senior leadership team and was 'seconded' into a service ownership role. To make it official, she was asked to apply and interview, following HR policy. Of course, Lucy was offered the role – meaning she was safe. The new senior leader, who was on a contract, had also been appointed to be the director of the newly formed department that Lucy just so happened to be working in. Lucy liked this new leader. She had all the traits of Amber but was just a nice person who had a fresh approach and saw talents across the department, she even tried to help Dre before he left.

It also felt inspirational to Lucy to have a female at director level making business decisions that made sense. Lucy knew that this was her opportunity to learn leadership the right way.

"Research shows women are interrupted or spoken [sic] 50% of the time while speaking in work meetings – and the culprits are usually men."[13]

[13] https://www.stylist.co.uk/life/careers/men-interrupting-women-work-meetings/457339.

CHAPTER 12: TALES OF REAL-WORLD ALLYSHIP

Scott

The thing with misogyny, felt Scott, was that once you saw it, you saw it everywhere. What was more, you felt compelled to fight it – and this was where it was easy to trip up.

Scott's boss Helen was the process owner of their area, and while female managers were no novelty in the company, some of the contractors were unused to women in authority.

During a recent governance meeting, Scott had lost his temper with a contractor who didn't seem to understand that Helen was in charge. The contractor had repeatedly rejected the premise of Helen's questions or directed his replies to Scott instead of her, even lecturing her about her own process at one point. Scott was furious and snapped at the contractor.

He knew straight away he had messed up. He had turned a discussion into a fight and, worst of all, he had made it about him. Helen called time on that meeting and in due course got the outcome she had wanted, but Scott felt he had made it harder for her by letting his emotions get the better of him.

Over the course of his career, Scott had learned that misogyny didn't just discriminate against women, it set an arbitrary standard for manhood and penalised those who didn't meet it. When competence was only considered after height, heterosexuality, a deep baritone and a golf club membership, it hurt everyone outside that privileged minority.

Therefore, Scott felt that when you saw misogyny play out in front of you, it was natural to respond emotionally, out of a sense of guilt by association with injustices inflicted on women, and out of indignation over the opportunities denied to people. But this was a mistake.

Giving in to that indignation felt like fighting back but in truth it denied agency to women. Scott decided that in future, he'd follow his own advice: "Take a breath. Don't react in anger. Change doesn't happen in war, it happens in peace."

Dave

Like a lot of people, Dave had a love-hate relationship with meetings. They were an inescapable part of the corporate world but posed challenges in ensuring everyone was treated fairly and respectfully.

Dave understood that noticing when someone was uncomfortable in a meeting could be challenging. The narrative around this was slowly changing, but genuine empathy often required having walked a mile in the other person's shoes.

Dave's organisation held meetings with people from various cultures and time zones. The problem with the relative anonymity of virtual calls was that people could become emboldened to display disrespectful behaviour.

During one such regular meeting, the typical scenario unfolded. The male host launched into an exhaustive slide deck, pausing only occasionally for questions. Despite the monotonous nature of such meetings, Dave believed that some behaviours of hosts or attendees were inexcusable.

With around 35 participants, most attendees stayed quiet. The host and those responding to questions were predominantly male, which skewed the dynamics significantly.

A critical moment came when a team member, whose insight Dave had always valued, raised an important question. The host ignored the question, continuing to the next slide without missing a beat.

It could have been a technical glitch or that the host hadn't heard the question or was planning to circle back to it later. But Dave was doubtful. This wasn't the first time it had happened; in fact, Dave had noticed a distinct pattern emerging where the questions and contributions of male colleagues were taken seriously and those of female colleagues were dismissed or outright ignored.

At the moment, Dave didn't ponder the reasons — only the blatant disrespect registered. As the host began discussing the next slide, Dave intervened.

"Excuse me, I think Joan had a question about the previous slide."

The host paused for a second then complied. Dave still off mute, said "Joan, I think you were asking about the project timelines here?"

"Great observation!" the host exclaimed.

"Actually, it isn't my observation, hence why I mentioned Joan has a question" Dave said. "And I would appreciate it if you could address her directly, as you seemed to be overlooking her!"

There might be excuses – perhaps the host hadn't heard the question, maybe there was a technical issue, or he was planning to circle back to it later. Dave, however, finds these to be inadequate justifications. Better behaviour is expected; indeed, everyone should strive for improvement.

Dave knew that he couldn't be certain the host hadn't heard the question the first time, but he felt pretty sure this was another case of bad behaviour simply because of his colleague's gender.

It wasn't always about gender, though. Sometimes, Dave saw this kind of dismissal when other protected characteristics were involved, like religious belief or skin colour. When such situations arose, he realised it was essential to stand together and support each other.

Allyship, as Dave was discovering, wasn't about a powerful figure defending a weaker one, it was about standing shoulder to shoulder as equals to eradicate prejudice and injustice across all walks of life.

Dave had never truly understood what it meant to be an ally until this incident, which marked the beginning of his journey in allyship.

"A new UN report has found almost 90% of men and women hold some sort of bias against females."

"The 'Gender Social Norms' index analysed biases in areas such as politics and education in 75 countries."

"Globally, close to 50% of men said they had more right to a job than women. Almost a third of respondents thought it was acceptable for men to hit their partners."[14]

"A staggering 76% of the respondents we asked said that they have experienced gender bias or discrimination in the workplace at least once."[15]

---

[14] *https://www.bbc.co.uk/news/world-51751915*.

[15] *https://www.womenintech.co.uk/6-reasons-why-so-many-women-leave-tech-jobs/*.

CHAPTER 13: WHY SO BIASED?

Lucy

Lucy was thrilled to be representing the Women's Network at her company's Diversity, Equity and Inclusion (DE&I) Employee Relations Group (ERG) community day with the DE&I team and three key members of the C-suite. One being the CEO.

The day started off well. Lucy had the opportunity to network with the other ERGs and to learn more about different communities, their goals and achievements. There was even some training on inclusive communication, at which Lucy eagerly wrote notes not just for the Women's Network but for her own content creation.

When it came to the time to present to the CEO, the chief people officer (CPO) and another C-suite member who Lucy wanted to say had something to do with business, she sat patiently waiting her turn. She was last to go, and thought 'save the best to last'.

Lucy observed, and curiously watched the other ERG leaders present who they were, what they do, what they have done and their ask. She watched the reaction of the C-suite and wrote notes of any questions they asked or challenges they posed. In the back of Lucy's mind, she thought that the CEO didn't quite get it but also gave him the benefit of the doubt that perhaps he was uncomfortable outside of a boardroom setting talking people instead of profit.

When it was Lucy's turn she introduced herself, explained what the Women's Network was and then explained her requests.

"I don't come with just one ask; I come with two," she began, noticing that the CEO wasn't looking at her as she spoke. "Firstly, we would love it if someone in the leadership team could engage with some of the Women's Network content or attend some of our events."

"OK, sure," the CEO nodded, though he didn't look very convinced.

"Secondly," Lucy continued, "we would like the support of a leadership programme for women in the organisation. According to the stats, more women are leaving the company then we are recruiting, and women only make up 1.5% of senior roles…"

"Oh, but we already offer great maternity cover…" the CPO interjected. As he went on to talk about it, Lucy shook her head.

The CEO, aware that Lucy wasn't impressed, said, "Ah, let's hear what she thinks," pointing at her.

Lucy paused, knowing that this needed to be handled well. "I hear your point," Lucy said slowly, matching the tone of the room. "The maternity pay here is the best in the industry and that's fantastic. But that's not what we're asking for."

The leadership team members – all male – frowned at Lucy. She knew she needed to educate them.

"What about the women who can't have children?" Lucy asked. "Or choose not to have children? Or have had their babies and are back on the career ladder wanting to progress? We have a lot of talented women here in this business, who are missing out on opportunities…"

"But what about the men?" the CEO interrupted. "We have lots of talented men who need to progress, too."

Lucy, feeling herself getting cross, her face flushed, reached for her glass of water. "Well, yes, I am not dismissing that. But I think you are missing the point I'm making."

The room fell silent.

The CEO, who clearly wasn't listening, started to talk about one of his executive team, who had recently come back from maternity leave. She had only taken two months off and was back at work. Could we not take inspiration from her?

"Absolutely not!" thought Lucy, stunned at the suggestion and wondering whether the woman in question had been pressurised into taking so little time off. Even though she didn't want a baby herself, Lucy was pretty sure this was a very unhealthy response from the CEO.

But Lucy wasn't quick enough to answer and her time was up.

She realised there and then that DE&I was a tick-box exercise for this particular brand.

Lucy

"Thing is, Luce…" Lucy cringed, she hated being called 'Luce'.

"…women don't want to do shift work."

"What makes you say that?" Lucy enquired.

"You know women need to pick up the kids, make the dinner and all that. Shift work is for men," Syed announced proudly.

Lucy frowned. "I think you're speaking to the wrong person about this."

Or maybe, Syed was speaking to the right person. It was this kind of behaviour and perhaps even culture in the workplace that wasn't helpful for women. How did you overcome it? How did you challenge a stereotype?

Lucy told her colleague Dave about the conversation.

Dave took a moment to digest the information. Both he and Lucy knew that Syed was about to join Dave's team.

"I think I have some educating to do," Dave replied. He had been working at the company longer that Lucy had been alive. And Lucy wasn't afraid to raise issues with him.

When Lucy had first met Dave, they had an instant connection. Dave understood Lucy. He could see her ambition and shared some stories of his own challenges as person of colour in the tech industry and from his childhood. Lucy enjoyed speaking to Dave because she got to be an ally herself. She was able to ask open questions and get open and honest answers back.

"So, what are we going to do?" Lucy asked.

"Leave it with me," Dave smiled. "I have an idea."

Akua

Akua was a highly skilled infrastructure analyst with more than six years of experience in financial services. She had to overcome numerous hurdles to get to where she was. Her journey was not an easy one, but allyship played a crucial role in her success.

After graduating from university, Akua found herself struggling to secure a role due to the financial recession and a lack of perceived experience. It took nearly two years before she finally landed a job, often being overlooked for male candidates or discriminated against because of her name, which suggested she wasn't English, despite being born in London. The struggle made her question whether the technology industry was right for her.

Throughout her career, Akua faced unexpected challenges. She was frequently pigeonholed into roles or asked to take on multiple responsibilities, including secondments, without ever being offered a permanent position in a higher role. This knocked her confidence, despite her dedication, overtime hours and commitment to taking on projects to prove her willingness to learn. Her stellar performance and innovative contributions were often overshadowed by subtle moments of sexism in the workplace.

At one point, Akua had proposed an idea to streamline the onboarding process. Having successfully implemented a similar process at a previous job, she was confident in her proposal. However, during an initial meeting, a colleague dismissed her suggestions. Instead of giving constructive feedback, her male colleagues were dismissive and patronising. Comments like, "Are you sure this is the correct method?" and "Maybe we should run this by one of the guys" abounded. The worst one came from a senior manager who said his "monkey brain could not take so many emails". Akua found this extremely offensive, and while she received an apology, the moment left a lasting impact.

Despite these challenges, Akua continued to excel in her work, surpassing expectations and working hard on her yearly objectives. However, the glass ceiling remained unyielding. Promotions went to less experienced counterparts, and management often hired external male candidates rather than nurturing internal talent. Feeling frustrated but determined, Akua decided to address the issue head-on.

13: Why so biased?

She scheduled a meeting with her manager, listed her points of concern, and discussed her achievements, the positive impact of her work and her aspirations for career growth. Her manager, unaware of the subtle biases within the team, listened and agreed to support her more in meetings. Although immediate changes were limited, this led to a review of job titles and grades within her division by the global director and head of her division. The progress was ongoing but positive, leading to a pay rise and bonus in the meantime. Additionally, the company committed to organising diversity and inclusion workshops to raise awareness and foster a more inclusive work environment.

Over time, the workplace culture began to shift. Akua's contributions were recognised and she was included as a key contributor in meetings with management. The company's commitment to addressing sexism not only benefited Akua but also created a more inclusive atmosphere for everyone. Empowered to speak up against sexism, Akua helped pave the way for positive change within the organisation. She helped in developing, structuring and providing content for unconscious bias training with the learning and development team, thanks to a mentor who supported and advocated for her.

Reflecting on her journey, Akua realised the importance of seeking out mentors, a sentiment endorsed by notable female's such as United States politician Kamala Harris and ex-first lady of the United States Michelle Obama, who emphasised having more than one mentor. Initially, Akua lacked the confidence to reach for big goals. However, over time, she removed self-doubt through daily affirmations and focused on her passions. She also learned to be open to multiple possibilities while focusing on the present.

13: Why so biased?

Akua started leaning on her communities, friends, sponsors and advocates to help her drive change. They picked her up when she was falling and demonstrated true allyship, allowing her to rise above the challenges and achieve success in her career.

Lucy, Dave, Akua

When Dave first learned about the battles Akua was facing at the company, he saw parallels with his own experiences and recognised an opportunity for allyship. He reached out to her, offering support and sharing insights from his own battles against workplace discrimination. Akua's initiative helped kickstart diversity and inclusion workshops, and together with Dave, the two began to shape a more supportive culture at their company. Dave had been with the company for decades, long enough to see its culture morph several times over. But some old habits, as they say, die hard. This was evident the day Lucy, one of his newer colleagues, came to him troubled by a conversation she had just had with another team member, Syed.

"Thing is Luce," Syed had started using the nickname Lucy despised. "Women don't want to do shift work."

Lucy, taken aback by the casual sexism, had replied, "What makes you say that?"

"You know, women need to pick up the kids, make the dinner and all that. Shift work is for men," Syed proudly announced.

Lucy, unamused and perturbed, had countered, "I think you are speaking to the wrong person about this."

Perhaps Syed was indeed speaking to the right person as this kind of archaic mindset needed challenging, especially in the modern workplace. Lucy had immediately sought out Dave, his experience and wisdom would be invaluable in addressing this issue.

Dave listened intently as Lucy relayed the conversation, his expression one of concern but not surprise. He took a moment to digest the information, well aware that Syed was soon to be transferred to his team.

"I think I have some educating to do," Dave remarked, a determined look crossing his face. Lucy smiled, reassured by his response. Dave's history in the tech industry as a person of colour had given him a unique insight into the nuances of workplace discrimination. He had shared stories with Lucy about his own challenges and triumphs, which not only showcased his resilience but also made him a relatable and trusted mentor.

"Leave it with me," Dave said with a knowing smirk. "I have an idea."

Meanwhile, Akua, a skilled infrastructure analyst at the company, faced her own set of challenges. Despite having over six years of experience and a solid educational background, she struggled with the subtle biases that frequently undercut her contributions. From being overlooked for promotions to dealing with dismissive comments during meetings, Akua's journey was a testament to the resilience required to navigate such an environment.

One particular incident had left a deep impression on her. During a team meeting, she had suggested an innovative approach to streamline the onboarding process, an idea based on a successful strategy she had implemented in a previous role. Instead of engaging with her proposal, her colleagues questioned its validity with one senior manager offensively remarking that his "monkey brain could not take so many emails."

Although Akua received an apology for the remark, the damage was done. It revealed the pervasive sexism she had to contend with, propelling her to take a stand. She scheduled a meeting with her manager and meticulously prepared her case highlighting her achievements, overlooked contributions and firmly requested more support in meetings.

This proactive approach eventually led to some positive changes. Her manager became more attentive and the division head initiated a review of job titles and grades which culminated in a pay rise and a bonus for Akua. Moreover, her initiative helped kickstart diversity and inclusion workshops aimed at fostering a more inclusive work environment.

After Lucy joined the business, the three formed a trio of advocates for change. They collaborated on developing unconscious bias training, and their efforts slowly transformed the workplace dynamics. Their allyship was not about speaking for each other but amplifying each other's voices, challenging outdated norms, and ensuring that everyone, regardless of gender or background, was given a fair chance to succeed.

Meanwhile, Dave needed to address the issue of Syed.

As Dave prepared for Syed's transition to his team, he knew that Syed's problematic views needed a nuanced and educational approach. Dave believed that meaningful change could best be achieved through empathy and dialogue rather than confrontation.

Dave began by arranging a series of one-on-one discussions with Syed, focusing on the company's values around diversity and inclusion. These conversations were designed to gently challenge Syed's preconceptions and encourage self-reflection. Dave's approach was patient and supportive, aiming to guide Syed rather than reproach him.

To give Syed a deeper understanding of the impacts of exclusionary attitudes, Dave organised workshops that included role-playing exercises. These were structured to place Syed in the shoes of colleagues who felt marginalised, an experience that proved eye-opening for him. Through these role-play activities, Syed began to empathise with those on the receiving end of comments he had made.

Lucy, played a vital part in his education. She engaged in direct dialogue with Syed, sharing her own experiences and the challenges she faced as a woman in tech. Lucy's candidness helped Syed grasp the personal impact of his assumptions and sparked a genuine reconsideration of his views.

As Syed's understanding grew, Akua joined the effort. Her own journey of overcoming subtle workplace biases offered another layer of depth to the discussions. Akua shared specific instances where biases had hindered her career progression, helping Syed see the broader implications of such attitudes within the tech industry. Her involvement reinforced the importance of considering diverse perspectives and challenged Syed to further question his own biases.

Encouraged by his interactions with Lucy and Akua, Syed became increasingly reflective and open to change. He started to actively participate in diversity and inclusion initiatives at the company and sought ways to support these efforts beyond mere compliance.

13: Why so biased?

Several months later, during a company-wide meeting, Syed took the opportunity to share his personal transformation. He publicly acknowledged his past misconceptions and thanked Lucy and Akua for their crucial roles as allies in his journey. His speech, which detailed his process of unlearning and relearning, not only marked his growth but also highlighted the powerful impact of allyship within the workplace.

Syed's transformation showcased how the combined efforts of colleagues acting as allies could foster significant personal and organisational change. By working together, Lucy, Akua and Dave helped cultivate a more inclusive environment, demonstrating that allyship involves not just support for those marginalised but also education and growth for those who are learning to understand their impact on others.

"85% of our female respondents say there's a gender disparity within their team."[16]

---

[16] *https://www.skillsoft.com/2024-women-in-tech-report.*

CHAPTER 14: HORRIBLE BOSSES 2

Lucy

Lucy's phone pinged. It was an email from Roseanna Peters.

Roseanna Peters – where did Lucy know that name from? Within seconds, she remembered. It was Rose, a woman she had hired at a previous company. "I wonder what she wants. I hope she's OK!" Lucy thought as she opened the email.

Rose's message was friendly yet professional, asking if they could catch up. Lucy knew immediately that something was wrong. She assumed it was to do with the mass redundancies Rose's company was going through, though Lucy sensed it was more than that.

Lucy had hired Rose as a career returner, following a break from paid work. Knowing that the business was embarking on a large transformational project, Lucy had asked to see the career returner in-house programme. But there was none. She had worried at the time that this was bad news for people like Rose. "We don't set people up for success here!" she had vented at her colleagues. "We hire talented people and we don't support them!"

Lucy sent Rose a text, telling her to call any time.

A few days later, Lucy's phone rang.

"Hi Rose," Lucy answered. They exchanged the usual pleasantries until Lucy ventured, "Are you OK Rose? What's up?"

Rose muffled her words and rambled. Then she asked, "Did you leave because of the boss?"

Lucy answered immediately. Usually cautious with her words, she knew that this was the time to be truthful.

Lucy didn't leave just because of the boss, Jules, but he was a deciding factor. Upon joining the company, Lucy and Jules got on well. He understood her aspirations and was supportive of her plans to eventually move away from PAYE to launch her own venture.

With the huge changes in the business, Lucy's job had changed a lot. Her role had narrowed into doing just data analysis, which wasn't a key strength of hers. Other roles around her had changed too, and the business wasn't the same as when she started there.

But yes, Lucy did have moments with Jules that made her incredibly miserable. He once made her sit on a one-to-one Teams call with him for five hours while he did a report. She sat in silence, feeling stressed and confused. He would gaslight her and question her character. The worst moment was when he used her mental health situation as an example of poor performance.

Lucy wasn't the first woman to have had this experience with Jules. He once said to her Polish colleague, that she needed to work on her accent because people didn't understand her. Then there was Kim. It wasn't overly clear what had happened, but upon the first meeting Lucy had with her, Kim told Lucy that the 'blocker for a career' was having Jules as a boss.

Rose explained the situation that she was in. As predicted, she hadn't had any support upon joining and she told a familiar story of her first few weeks.

"I'm so sorry to hear this, Rose," Lucy began. "I'm happy to chat with you about it but I'm not overly sure what I can do to support you as I am no longer at the company."

Rose asked if Lucy had reported Jules's behaviour. She had in a way, but only via confidential conversations with Jules's boss and then in her exit interview. The truth was, this chap had been in the business since he left university and 20 years on, he had navigated and curated a career path for himself. The directors loved him and he had a good track record. Aside from all this, he was technically very good and also when in the right mood, a good manager.

Lucy suggested that Rose speak to the manager above Jules about Lucy's exit notes and have a confidential conversation with him to explain that she was having similar problems.

Rose nonetheless felt defeated and the last message she sent to Lucy read:

I think it would just be easier if I left.

Lucy didn't reply.

A few months later, Rose texted Lucy again with an update:

I decided to leave.

Lucy didn't reply. Again. Mainly because she didn't know what to say. Should she had got more involved? Or was she right to protect herself?

Either way, Lucy had tried to help where she could. Being in an industry that is so small and where people do gossip – she just knew that sometimes there was a line between protecting others and looking out for yourself.

"A staggering 56% of women leaving the tech industry 10-20 years into their careers, which is double the rate of men."[17]

[17] *https://www.womenintech.co.uk/6-reasons-why-so-many-women-leave-tech-jobs/*.

CHAPTER 15: FEELING STUCK

Lucy

"I don't want to do this role," Lucy confessed to Dave.

"That's because you're meant to be a business owner. I can see you owning your own company one day," Dave replied.

Lucy was looking down at her feet. Her red-painted toes were poking out of her limited-edition tan leather sandals. She was feeling stuck in a rut. She had turned to Dave after another particularly challenging day after an unwanted role change. She was feeling a bit bitter about it all. And she really didn't want to keep doing data analysis.

Dave had recognised the signs. He had got to know Lucy pretty well and he knew the type of people that she was dealing with in their team. Dave knew Lucy was too good for the role and although he didn't want to see her leave, he couldn't let her waste her talent and purpose number-crunching in a failing business.

Dave took a moment and then said, "Have you considered launching something of your own?"

Lucy, holding a lukewarm bitter coffee, replied, "Yes, I'm already doing something of my own and I have all these ideas, but I don't know where to start."

"Can I share some advice?"

"Err…yes!" Lucy leaned in towards Dave.

"I have run a number of businesses. Some have worked out, some haven't, and some have cost me more than they made me."

Dave cleared his throat.

"I think you need to take a risk. And trust that whatever happens, it will all work out for the best. You can't stay working here. Well you can, but you'll be wasted. You'll be unhappy. Lucy – you are destined for bigger and better things."

Lucy knew what Dave was saying. She knew what she needed to do.

David

David stood beneath the towering spectacle of the Gherkin in the heart of London, a symbolic illustration of the city's global reach, its finance and ambition. The Gherkin reflected not just the bustling metropolis but the myriad of thoughts and decisions that had brought David to this point in his life. Having navigated the intricate world of IT Service Management for nearly two decades, serving some of the industry's most illustrious companies and clients, David was no stranger to success. Yet, a persistent, quiet voice had been nudging him towards a different kind of path. He felt stuck. He also felt impeded by a glass ceiling that he didn't have the energy to smash through.

For ten years, that voice had competed with more familiar choruses – those singing the virtues of job security and steady pay packets. But the tune changed abruptly one day, thanks to a revealing glance at the company's billing statements. Added to the negative company culture, this was hard to stomach. In unapologetic bold figures, David saw the amount his employer charged clients for his services. The numbers were eye-watering, and not just because he hadn't had his morning mocha yet. David couldn't help but laugh; he'd been selling champagne services on a beer budget!

This revelation came during a particularly precarious time in his career – a probationary period in a new role that had a potential six-month exit clause in the contract. The irony wasn't lost on David. Here he had been, fretting about job security while his own talents were being traded like precious metals. The probation had been less of a safety net and more of a tightrope, and yet when it came to the probation interview, after repeated requests for it, it was bypassed by a simple email saying it was a slam dunk. It left him no opportunity to discuss the terrible onboarding or the awful company culture.

With the Gherkin standing stoically in the background, David made his decision. He wouldn't wait for the official probation verdict. He would take his skills and invest them in his own venture. David crafted his resignation letter with a blend of earnest gratitude and barely contained excitement. He thanked his boss for the "invaluable insights into his own billing rate" and left with a flourish that left his colleagues whispering in the break room for weeks.

The journey from a secure job to the rocky road of consultancy and entrepreneurship was peppered with challenges that would have sent many back to the safety of employment. But David, armed with years of experience and a new-found confidence, tackled each obstacle as if it were a minor glitch in a system he was programmed to debug. David also hated to admit failure, so he dug in and took a step forward each day.

Securing clients was an exercise in humility and hustle. Every pitch was a reminder that he was no longer backed by a big name, just his own. This realisation was both terrifying and exhilarating. Managing finances turned into a daily game of Tetris, with David arranging his limited resources in the most efficient patterns possible.

Yet, every small victory was sweeter because it was truly his. David's company slowly carved out a niche in the competitive landscape of IT Service Management. Applying the skills that had made him a valuable employee, he now brought a personal touch to each project, treating each client's business as if it were his own, because, in a way, it now was. He began co-creating value, where others just applied value financially.

The moment of truth came one crisp autumn day when David received an invitation to lead a major project – inside the Gherkin itself. As he walked into the building, this time not as an employee but as the head of his own consulting firm, the sense of achievement was overwhelming. The Gherkin wasn't just a building; it was a monument to his journey – a journey of embracing the unknown and confronting his fears.

Working within the Gherkin, David not only co-created value for everyone involved, but also cemented his reputation as a leader in his field. The project was not just a professional victory; it was a personal triumph that echoed the decision made years ago beneath this very glass dome.

It also provided his first business case that he could use to share his experiences with others. A spark was lit and a desire to share his story was born.

"Deloitte researchers found that only 59% of women who said they were harassed reported the incidents to their employer, down from 66% in the prior year's survey." [18]

---

[18] https://www.bbc.com/worklife/article/20230615-why-its-getting-harder-for-some-women-to-report-harassment.

CHAPTER 16: HANDLING 'IT'

Lyra

"There is one more thing I need to speak to you about." Lyra was on the video call for her one-to-one with her new boss.

"Do you know Arun, the chap that works on the service desk for Jai?" Lyra asked.

Martin looked up, trying to recall the name. "Oh yeah, Arun," he said after a pause.

"Well," Lyra began. "I feel a bit embarrassed mentioning this and it hasn't happened to me in a long time…"

Lyra took a deep breath.

"Well, every time I speak to Arun face to face, he doesn't look at my *face*, if you get my drift. And aside from the fact that it is annoying me and it is just so rude – I am worried that he could do it to someone else who isn't as confident as me… Do you know what I mean?"

Martin's eyes widened. "Oh," he said.

There was silence.

"And I was just wondering if I could get some advice on how to handle it?" Lyra asked.

As a natural reflector, Martin paused, not really knowing what to do and not really wanting to have this on his plate. "I'm happy to speak to Jai, if you want me to. But I know you've established a good relationship with Jai, so why don't you speak to him about it and I'll mention it to him too when we have our catch up in the week?"

"Sure," Lyra said, disappointed that Martin wasn't going to do much about it. But in a way, he had a point: she was getting on really well with Jai and they often went for a coffee, so she would just tell him next time she saw him.

"I'll speak to him, Lyra, no worries," Jai promised.

"Don't – you know – make it into a big thing," Lyra said. "I have to work with him and I don't want him to be funny with me or anything."

"Nah, leave it with me," Jai reassured her. "I'm just going to say he can't do that. He can't be disrespectful like that. I'm going to tell him that I have seen him do it, which I am embarrassed to say, I have with a girl on his team – and he can't be doing that. Especially with someone like you. You're at least two grades higher than him. In fact, he shouldn't be doing that full stop. To anyone." Jai was annoyed that anyone in his team would behave this way and also damage the brand of the team he had built and fought for.

"Thanks, Jai. Sorry to put you in this position."

"Don't be sorry. We're pals; I've got you," Jai said. "Even if we weren't, I would still be having this conversation with him," Jai clarified.

Arun never looked at Lyra's chest again. In fact, his whole behaviour changed. Lyra didn't know if it was something that Jai had said, all she knew was that Jai had her back – he'd taught Arun some manners and potentially 'saved' other women from being gawked at.

"According to the Sutton Trust, 80% of editors went to private school; only 11% of journalists are from working-class backgrounds, and a measly 0.2% of journalists are Black."[19]

---

[19] https://www.theguardian.com/media/2024/apr/04/new-journalism-school-in-london-sets-out-to-improve-black-representation.

CHAPTER 17: B*TCH

Samantha

Samantha collapsed onto the couch with a sigh, clutching a steaming mug of tea, her eyes scanning the cluttered living room that she shared with her housemate, Lucy. The twinkling lights of their modest Christmas tree flickered in the corner, casting a soft glow over the dimly lit space. Lucy, sprawled across the armchair with a novel in hand, looked up, her expression softening as she noticed the fatigue on Samantha's face.

"What's wrong, Sam?" Lucy's voice was tinged with concern as she bookmarked her page and set the novel aside.

"It's just...the Christmas party," Samantha started, her voice trailing off as she searched for the right words. The memories of the evening were still fresh, the words that had been thrown at her still stinging. She took a deep breath, steadying herself before diving into the story.

"You know I got promoted to the news desk, right? Well, at the party, this woman from marketing – someone I've never even spoken to – comes up to me after a few drinks and says, "Everyone thinks you must be a b*tch to have gotten that job, but I actually think you're quite nice."" Samantha's voice was a mix of disbelief and frustration.

Lucy's brow furrowed. "She said what? That's awful, Sam. I'm so sorry."

Samantha shook her head, a bitter laugh escaping her lips. "It's like, no matter what you do, it's never about your skills or the hard work. It's always some petty judgement or other.

And what's worse, it's this double standard. If I were a guy, they'd just say I was ambitious, right? But no, I have to be a 'bitch' or somehow manipulative."

Lucy nodded. "It's that old cliché, isn't it?" she responded. "Men are assertive; women are bossy. Men are strategic; women are scheming. It's exhausting."

"Exactly!" Samantha exclaimed, setting her mug down with a clatter. "And you know what the irony is? This job, working in journalism – it was never a given for me. I didn't start in some cushy internship my parents snagged through connections. I fought to get here, from that council estate in Paulsgrove all the way to the news desk."

Lucy listened intently as Samantha recounted her journey – the years of overcoming social and economic hurdles, from witnessing poverty and violence in her youth to navigating the elitist terrain of the media. Samantha spoke of the gruelling hours, the second jobs she worked to afford her education, and the demeaning assumptions people made about her based on her background and appearance.

"The thing is, Lucy," Samantha continued, her voice growing firmer, "I want to do things differently. I've seen editors scream and belittle their staff, and it achieves nothing but fear and resentment. I want to lead with respect, to prove that you don't have to lose your humanity to be successful in this industry."

Lucy reached out, squeezing Samantha's hand. "And you will, Sam. You're one of the strongest, kindest people I know. You're going to change things, I'm sure of it."

Samantha smiled, the warmth from Lucy's words soothing some of the sting from earlier. "Thanks, Lu. It means a lot to hear that, especially today. It's just so frustrating sometimes, feeling like you're constantly having to prove yourself not just as a professional, but as a decent human being."

They sat in silence for a moment, the only sound the soft crackling of the Christmas playlist in the background. Then, Lucy stood up, walking over to the tiny kitchenette.

"You know what we need? A proper girls' night. Let's open that bottle of wine we've been saving, order the greasiest pizza we can find, and just vent. All this bullshit isn't going anywhere, but tonight, let's just be us."

Samantha laughed. "That sounds perfect!"

"When I was 23, I was working as a cashier at a retail store. I had finished closing my till for the night, so I asked my 36-year-old manager what else I could do to help close the store. He answered, 'Don't worry. Just keep standing there and looking pretty, that's what you're good for.'"

"I was actively having a miscarriage at work, and when I realized what was happening, I left to go to the emergency room. I only took one day off to process. Within the first hour of coming back to work, a man from my department walked by my desk and very loudly said, 'Nice of you to show up.' My jaw hit the floor. Most of the office knew, but even if he didn't, it was absolutely none of his business."[20]

[20] https://www.buzzfeed.com/victoriavouloumanos/worst-thing-men-have-said-to-women-at-work-5.

CHAPTER 18: ARE MEN SAYING THE WRONG THINGS?

David

David walked back to his desk, his Grenson boots squeaking on the office tiles as they had retained dampness from the cobbles outside. As always at 08:30, David held a mocha in one hand with the other glued to his phone, though this morning he was feeling embarrassed.

He had just returned from the local Pret, where he had run into one of this clients Samantha, who looked particularly stylish that day. Her outfit was fantastic – a combination of elegance and confidence that caught his attention.

As he admired her attire, he was struck by an unexpected internal debate – should he comment on her outfit or keep his thoughts to himself? In the end, he stumbled into a "You look, I mean, great shoes" type of comment before scuttling off.

The moment lingered in his mind. He knew that giving compliments was a common social gesture, but he was acutely aware of the fine line between a genuine compliment and coming across as inappropriate or unprofessional. He was genuinely impressed by Samantha's outfit, but he didn't want his words to be misconstrued as an attempt to cross boundaries.

David had always prided himself on treating those he worked with, with respect and fairness. He valued the professional relationships he had built over the years and didn't want to jeopardise them. He knew that navigating these nuances was essential, especially when it came to acknowledging someone's appearance.

During a coffee break, he decided to seek advice from someone he could trust, Sophie. Sophie was known for being sensitive to workplace dynamics and for her respectful approach to conversations.

"Hey, Sophie," David started, "I had a bit of a situation earlier. I wanted to compliment Samantha on her outfit, but I'm worried it might have come across the wrong way."

Sophie sipped her coffee thoughtfully. "Compliments can be tricky, especially in a professional setting. The key is to make sure your intention is clear and your words are respectful."

David nodded, his curiosity piqued. "So, how do you strike that balance?"

Sophie smiled knowingly. "First, make sure your compliment is specific and focused on something work-appropriate. If you're praising her outfit, emphasise the professional aspect – the colour choice, the style or how it complements the occasion."

"That makes sense," David said. "Is it also about being genuine with your sentiment?"

"Exactly," Sophie agreed. "And also, consider the context and the existing rapport you have with the person. If your interactions have always been respectful and professional, your intentions are likely to be interpreted correctly."

Encouraged by Sophie's insights, David decided to approach the situation thoughtfully. When he next saw Samantha, he took a deep breath and approached her.

"Hey, Samantha," he said with a warm smile. "I have to say, your outfit today is fantastic. The colour suits you really well, and it's perfect for the work environment."

Samantha's eyes lit up with appreciation. "Thank you, David. I appreciate that."

As the day went on, David found himself reflecting on the interaction. He realised that his words hadn't only been about acknowledging Samantha's outfit; they were also a reflection of his respect for her professionalism and her contributions to the programme they were working on. It wasn't about objectifying her or implying anything beyond a friendly observation.

However, David's concerns still lingered in the back of his mind. He wondered whether Samantha or anyone else who might have overheard their conversation would think he was only seeing her as a potential date. He was reminded of the importance of context and the need to maintain consistent behaviour to avoid misunderstandings.

That evening, David shared his thoughts with his friend Zoe, who was a seasoned HR professional in her own field. She listened attentively as he expressed his concerns.

"Different people interpret things differently, David," Zoe said gently. "But remember that a single compliment doesn't define your entire reputation. It's your consistent behaviour and actions that matter."

David nodded, taking in her words. "So, it's about building a reputation of respect over time."

Zoe smiled. "Exactly. If your actions and interactions consistently align with professionalism and respect, a genuine compliment is less likely to be misinterpreted."

As the weeks went on, David continued to navigate his professional relationships with care. He learned that compliments when offered thoughtfully and respectfully, could enhance the workplace environment. It wasn't just about acknowledging someone's appearance, but about recognising their contributions to the workplace, not just in terms of objectives but also things like their teamwork and their communication and working towards creating a culture of mutual respect.

David's journey taught him that while it was important to be aware of potential misconceptions, it was equally important to be authentic, consistent and respectful whether that was complimenting an outfit or a work project, David actively chose not to let fear hinder genuine and positive interactions.

"One in 10 (10 per cent) employees have witnessed or experienced sexual harassment at work but half (49 per cent) of these do not report it."
"The survey of 2,000 employees by Personio also found that almost a third (30 per cent) of employees had seen or experienced bullying at work, but more than two in five (44 per cent) had not reported it."
"Of those surveyed, 43 per cent said they were worried about retaliation or retribution if they were to report an issue, compared to 56 per cent of employees who felt confident that sensitive workplace misconduct situations would be treated properly and fairly by their organisation."[21]

---

[21] *https://www.peoplemanagement.co.uk/article/1866611/half-employees-not-report-workplace-sexual-harassment-survey-finds-%E2%80%93-businesses-encourage-speaking-up.*

CHAPTER 19: ARE WE STILL EXPERIENCING THIS?

Lyra

Lyra had left her job and started contract-consulting, which was completely outside her comfort zone. But the lack of opportunities out there had meant she had to try something new.

Lyra had gone from working in general offices to working in a medical environment. To her surprise, she was very much enjoying it. The team she was aligned to would write down her suggestions – in fact they would write down literally *everything* she said. She had to pinch herself to believe that she, Lyra Bloom, was a consultant on whose words people hung.

Doing contract consulting, Lyra was involved in things she never dreamed she would do. She was writing corporate communications, mapping out potential large-scale business changes and even being invited to join client companies as an employee.

Lyra wasn't the only woman in this particular team. Or the 'woman in tech' – for the first time in her career. She was Lyra the subject matter expert. The professional. For once, her gender wasn't even part of the conversation.

Lyra was invited to a company-wide, in-person town hall meeting, where the project team would be presenting. In truth, Lyra wasn't too sure if this was the best use of her day rate but agreed to go.

19: Are we still experiencing this?

Lyra queued with the team to enter the lecture theatre, surrounded by analysts, doctors and board members. She took a moment to look around and appreciate where she was.

Lyra liked fashion and today she had her Ted Baker swing dress on, which was black, purple and green. Tights, court shoes and a Ted Baker coat in beige completed her outfit. People stared at Lyra, especially those who hadn't seen her before. This didn't trouble her too much as she was used to it. She knew she dressed differently to the crowd she was in. Lyra had worked very hard to craft her image and wasn't prepared to dress down to suit others.

On rare occasions, however, this could draw attention from the wrong people. And today was one such rare occasion.

As Lyra wandered down the aisle to find a seat near the front, an older man turned round and looked her up and down. He licked his lips, turned to his colleague and said loudly, "Cor...look at her! They don't make them like that anymore. Gorgeous. Over my knee!"

Horrified, Lyra froze. In her head, the following words kept spinning: "You're on a client site, calm down. YOU ARE ON A CLIENT SITE, CALM DOWN."

Lyra didn't know what to do. She wanted to say something but didn't want to appear unprofessional. Her face went red, she huddled over and swallowed the lump in her throat. The truth was, Lyra wanted to cry. She wanted to put her coat back on and run out of the door.

Instead, Lyra moved seats. She sat upright, listened and supported her project team.

As she walked back to the office, Lyra caught the eye of a senior leader she had been supporting.

19: Are we still experiencing this?

"Mateo," Lyra called. "Could I have a word?" Mateo was a reticent man but could see the look of concern on Lyra's face. She relayed the incident and then clearly outlined what she wanted to happen next:

"I'd like the chap spoken to, please, and I'd like him to be reminded that it isn't the 70's any more. He is entitled to his thoughts, but he needs to keep them to himself."

Mateo apologised, looking upset that his consultant was clearly shaken by what had happened. He made a mental note to do an investigation on the man in question and to make sure he hadn't done this to anyone else. Lyra clearly didn't want an apology, she just wanted to flag and problem solve. "A true professional," he thought.

That night on the train home, Lyra called her best friend and told her about it. Her friend knew that this would have upset Lyra, but offered some words of advice.

"I think you handled it well, Lyra. And I know this isn't the first time it has happened to you. You did everything you could, and if you are happy with how you handled it, then you did the right thing."

Lyra was silent. She felt that she should have reacted straight away to the man's sexist behaviour, but there were times and places for that. She was never one to make a scene but liked to tackle things professionally and promptly. And she did.

"According to a 2020 government survey of sexual harassment, 29% of those surveyed reported experiencing some form of sexual harassment in their workplace or work-related environment in the last 12 months."

"And it is no doubt that the issue is predominantly – but by no means completely – gendered. Almost two thirds (63%) of those who experienced sexual harassment in the workplace in the previous 12 months reported that the perpetrator was a man. Further to that, 81% of the women surveyed reported being harassed by a man."[22]

---

[22] *https://www.glamourmagazine.co.uk/article/new-statistics-about-sexual-harassment-in-the-workplace*.

CHAPTER 20: THE OFFSITE MEETING

Russell

Russell knew he was well endowed. And he wasn't shy about letting those around him know it, too. He made gestures by flexing his muscles or told people he was 'gifted'.

The office all roared with laughter when Russell made his comments. He appeared to be a great guy who helped people out and was on the side of those who weren't as privileged. He told Joe to stop talking over Jane in meetings and to stop asking her to take the minutes, and he attended the Black Lives Matter march in London with his Black and Asian colleagues. His jokey banter all seemed quite innocent. Until one day, it wasn't.

"I'll come and pick you up if you like?" Russell said to Lyra. "That way, we can car share and adhere to the company's green policy."

Russell and Lyra were off to a client site. Lyra hadn't been there before as she had recently began consulting on a freelance basis, so she appreciated Russell offering to collect her. They agreed on 6 am, so they would miss the M25 traffic and then grab a coffee and some breakfast before the day of client workshops and meetings began.

Russell, in his new car, arrived on the dot. Lyra, also an early bird, was ready. She grabbed her oxblood Mulberry bag, slipped on her Chanel style pumps and grabbed her blazer.

"Morning!" she sang as she hopped in the car.

"Morning, co-pilot!" Russell sang back.

The journey was smooth. They chatted about weekend plans, workshop plans, strategy and career aspirations. Because the conversation was so easy, the time passed quickly. They soon arrived at the client site and Russell parked his car, out of the way, hidden by trees.

"It's a sought-after car," Russell eye-rolled at Lyra.

Lyra understood; she used to date a guy who had been car obsessed. She knew that Audi sports cars were sometimes tampered with for their badges, or even stolen.

The day was just like any other client meeting and was a roaring success. The client loved the workshops Russell delivered and Lyra was able to get them to sign with the company for another three years, securing a deal worth £2.6 million. Lyra was already planning how to spend the commission in her head.

Buzzing, they both chattered and laughed as they headed back to the car. Russell playfully nudged Lyra, who pulled a silly face in return. They both felt high on their success. Lyra put her bag in the footwell, jumped in and said in a cool tone, "Ready, pilot? Let's tackle the M25."

Russell looked back at her. His face was a little different. He nodded down to his lower body; in his hand, he held his erect penis.

"Go on, touch it if you like," he said, his voice steady. "Look how big I am. I know you want to touch it."

Lyra froze. As if someone had a grip around her vocal cords, she couldn't speak, her heart pounding. Eventually, she was able to whisper, "No. I don't want to."

"You sure? Could be your only opportunity..." he began.

Russell looked up and saw the fear on Lyra's face. His original excitement turned into worry. He didn't say anything else, tidied himself away and popped on his seatbelt. He turned on the engine to start the journey home.

Lyra turned away and looked out of the window. A tear rolled down her cheek. She was trapped. She felt unsafe. Her phone in her bag, she was in shock and couldn't move.

Russell interrupted the silence by talking cheerily about the workshop. "Oh, then Geoff was saying how actually they could do with some consulting days and I suggested that maybe they speak to you? That workshop today, it's surprising isn't it, how some businesses just don't know their options. Did you say that Hilary signed up for another three years?"

"Yes," Lyra whispered back, still looking out of the window, wishing she had a superpower where she could snap her fingers and be back home.

Lyra

The journey felt like the longest journey of Lyra's life. As soon as Russell pulled up to her house, she grabbed her bag and rushed out of the car. Luckily, her housemate was already home, so the front door was unlocked. She ran in, locked the door and bolted it shut.

She didn't tell her housemate what had happened. She just told her she was tired and needed to sleep.

She hadn't planned to go to the office the next day but she did. She needed to tell someone what had happened. As she walked through the door towards her desk, she heard, "Morning, co-pilot!"

20: The offsite meeting

Lyra turned around in a panic, smiled and said, "Oh, morning…"

Her manager Robert was already in.

"Rob," Lyra whispered. "Can we have a chat please? Now."

Rob could see something was wrong. "Sure, let's get a coffee."

Lyra relayed the whole event to Rob. He sat in silence, sipped his coffee, then sipped it again.

"You sure that happened?" he asked. "Russ is a great guy. The clients love him – they're always requesting him for those workshops. Are you sure this wasn't a funny dream or something?"

"Why would I lie to you, Rob? This is my career!" Lyra said angrily.

"Well, OK. Don't tell anyone else. I will speak to him."

"You're not going to HR?"

"Nah," Rob said. "Useless bunch, that lot."

A week went by and it hadn't been mentioned again. Lyra didn't know what to do, but she had a colleague in another department, Wayne. They got on really well, with Wayne often entertaining Lyra with stories of his children and football. So Lyra decided to tell him.

"I'm going to punch him!" Wayne declared.

"Which one, Russell or Rob?" Lyra giggled. Wayne was such a good friend and ally.

"BOTH!"

20: The offsite meeting

"But, in all seriousness, what shall I do?" Lyra continued. "I have been assaulted."

"We need to go to HR. Today," Wayne decided.

Within an hour, Wayne had organised a confidential meeting with the HR business partner and the director of people.

Lyra repeated the story again.

"And you told Rob?" the director asked. "That surprises me."

"First of all, Lyra," started the HR business partner, who had been at the firm for 15 years. "Thank you for telling us." She tucked her mousy blonde hair behind her ear. "Tom and I will discuss the actions we need to take on this. I'm sorry to ask this–"

Here we go, Lyra thought.

"—Would you like to make this a police matter? Because this is indecent exposure and I also suspect this is sexual harassment and…had the potential to develop into a more sinister incident."

This shocked the room.

"I'll think about it," Lyra said. "I just couldn't live with myself if I hadn't told you this."

Tom, a late 20's man who had done well in his career, looked directly at Lyra and said, "I know this was hard for you, but thank you for telling us. Thank you for trusting us to handle this for you. Lyra if you need anything – time off or counselling – you let me know, OK?" Lyra nodded, looking at Tom who said "Lyra, work is unimportant right now, you do so much for our company, put yourself first."

Lyra smiled. "Thanks Tom. I'll be in touch."

20: The offsite meeting

Six weeks later

"I didn't see that one coming." The office gossip had started.

"Rob is retiring. Probably made too much money!" The interns were giggling.

Lyra had decided to report Russell to the police. After an investigation, he was terminated from his job with immediate effect and Lyra was informed that he had been put on some kind of register. Apparently, he had done this before at a previous company and there had been a big cover-up.

Tom, the director of people, held a company-wide global town hall meeting.

"I am here to announce that we are launching a number of people-focused programmes." He cleared his throat. "Every single person in this company will complete a sexual harassment training programme every year, like you do with your compliance training."

"Additionally, we have launched an allyship programme. This is where you can be part of a community to support people from all walks of life. We encourage you ALL to participate and complete the training."

Lyra smiled.

It wasn't easy to get this point, but she was proud of the changes that were being made because she had spoken up. She was able to make a difference thanks to Wayne. Without his allyship, it could have been a different story.

"Stalking is a crime that is experienced by both men and women, but the Crime Survey for England and Wales (CSEW) shows that women are more likely to be a victim."

"In the year ending March 2024, 1 in 25 (4%) women aged 16 years and over was a victim of stalking. In the same period, 2.3% of men were a victim."[23]

---

[23] *https://www.ons.gov.uk/peoplepopulationandcommunity/crimeandjustice/articles/ifeellikeiamlivingsomeoneelseslifeoneinsevenpeopleavictimofstalking/2024-09-26*.

CHAPTER 21: STALKER

Sophie

Sophie was working in a role where she needed to go regularly to the York office. This was a three-hour train journey that she undertook to meet with the team that she led. Before she travelled there the first time, Sophie's colleague Barry, who had been to the York office before, gave her directions and his mobile number in case she got stuck.

On that first trip, she crossed London by underground and was at the train station trying to figure out what platform she needed among the sea of flickering screens. She rang Barry from her personal mobile, her work one being buried too deep in her bag.

"Hi, Barry, I'm a little lost. Can you help figure out which platform I need to get to?"

She followed Barry's instructions, found the right train and arrived at the office without incident.

She had no idea that this one seemingly harmless request for help would be followed by 18 months of unwanted attention, sexual harassment and allyship from an unlikely candidate.

After getting to the York office that day, she had shared a joke with Barry.

"Thank you saving my tofu, Barry," Sophie laughed.

"No worries, Sophie. Glad you got here in one piece," Barry replied.

As it was an overnight trip, several colleagues were staying at the same hotel. They all checked in that evening and headed to their rooms with a plan to meet for dinner later.

Most people were on different floors except for Barry and Sophie, whose rooms were next to each other.

"No getting lost this time," Sophie quipped.

At dinner, there was the usual mix of business chatter and socialising. Sophie noticed that Barry kept looking over in her direction, but didn't give it much thought, instead focusing on enjoying the meal and chatting with the team.

Before it got too late, Sophie, leading by example, took the opportunity to retire to her room.

"Holy biscuits, my social battery is running out!" she said to Barry, who concurred and was ready for bed too. They shared the lift, chatting amiably and then went to their respective rooms.

Travelling back home the following day, Sophie found herself on the same train as Barry, so she sat next to him. She had dismissed the lingering looks from the night before and wanted to remain polite and professional.

As Sophie sat next to Barry at their London office, they knew each other slightly better than the standard water-cooler chat level, which helped pass the three-hour journey.

A couple of hours after arriving at her house, Sophie received a text message on her personal mobile from Barry.

> **It took all my willpower to stop myself from knocking on your hotel room door last night. I really wanted to spend the night with you.**

Shocked, Sophie blinked at the screen.

While her relationship status wasn't relevant to her colleagues, she had always been conscious of being in a male-dominated environment and wanted to ensure the boundaries were clear – so it was widely known in her department that she was in a long-term relationship. And in fact, she was sure that Barry also had a long-term partner.

> Sorry, Barry, I think we have our wires crossed here. I am not interested in having an office affair.

She hoped she had made it clear enough. She followed up with:

> • • •

> I'm sorry. I hope this isn't awkward now?

Barry responded.

> **Let's forget about it.**

Sophie breathed a sigh of relief.

Two weeks later, she was heading back to the York office and once again, Barry was on the same train. It was a day trip, so Sophie thought it unlikely that Barry could misread their interactions this time.

Always true to her word, Sophie acted as if Barry's advances had never happened. When she caught Barry staring at her again, she didn't say anything or react.

That night, Barry sent Sophie a message.

> **I do really like you. I have feelings for you.**

Again, she politely but firmly made her position clear, pointing out that writing to her like this, especially on her personal mobile, was inappropriate and had to stop.

Unfortunately, it didn't end there.

Over the next 12 months, Barry's advances continued, and they went beyond personal text messages.

He would send emails from his work address to hers with similar declarations, the subject heading tweaked each time:

Subject: Is it my imagination, you must like me because you're nice to me?

Subject: How can I be mistaken?

Subject: I can't stop thinking about you

Subject: I've had to move desks because being so close to you is driving me crazy

These emails would be essay-like in length. Barry would actively stare at her across the office. He would walk over to get involved in conversations she was having with others that were not within his role remit. He would ask to be involved in projects Sophie led and to join the meetings.

Barry's behaviour was clearly sexual harassment. And Sophie was being stalked.

"Why didn't you go to HR or tell your boss?" or "Why did you put up with it?" asked her friend Georgie when they met up for drink. Sophie had just finished telling her the whole story and showing her some of the messages.

"The truth is," Sophie began, "that I didn't know what to do."

Although Barry was horribly misguided about the situation, Sophie didn't want to get him in trouble, and she felt a little sorry for him as he just didn't seem to understand that being friendly wasn't the same as flirting.

She had also worked in IT for a long time and was concerned that the advances may be seen as harmless by her male leader or that she was overacting. Nor did she want her reputation to be tarred by reporting Barry or to be the subject of office gossip.

So instead, Sophie ignored the emails but kept them as evidence, restricted all her travel to the York office as day trips and didn't publicise when she was travelling to stop Barry from catching the same trains. In both offices, Sophie kept her distance from Barry as much as possible.

At no point was she scared but her patience wore thin very quickly, especially when Barry tried to contact Sophie on social media.

One of her boundaries in the workplace was to never interact on social media with colleagues, so Barry will have had to actively search for Sophie to contact her on Facebook and Instagram.

Sophie responded to Barry through a work email advising him to cease all contact with her besides those professional circumstances where interaction was warranted. She blocked him on all social media as well as on her personal mobile.

This latest attempt at contact removed the last trace of patience she had and resulted in a telephone call to her boss, Jonathan, to tell him what had been going on.

Jonathan was a middle-aged man who was not someone Sophie felt she could confide in. He was a pleasant person but she had never seen him show real empathy to others nor be an advocate for women in technology. Sophie didn't think her boss was sexist, but she realised his career had thrived in a male-dominated world and that he didn't appear to have the skills to relate to a woman's experience working in tech.

She told him everything that had happened but downplayed some of the harassment because she didn't want to be the cause of someone getting in trouble, or get an unfair reputation herself.

The outcome of the call was that she had found an ally in an unexpected quarter.

Jonathan was incredibly sympathetic, and showed true empathy and support. He said that she had to keep him informed of any further attempts from Barry to contact her, any unacceptable behaviour in the workplace and that he would keep a close eye on the office dynamics to ensure she was safe.

Sophie had requested that no action be taken because she assumed that her last contact with Barry had put a stop to the whole thing.

It hadn't.

The contact attempts from Barry outside of work reduced but she couldn't tell if that was because he had been blocked or because he was finally complying with her wishes.

Barry continued the attempts to speak to Sophie about spurious work-related matters at the office until Sophie lost her temper and publicly chastised him for wasting her time. It was so out of character, it left Sophie feeling ashamed.

The following morning, 18 months after the initial advance, Sophie finally met her breaking point.

She arrived at work, logged into her computer and opened her email to find a very long message from Barry with more advances and desperate attempts at emotional blackmail to get something from her, saying he had to move desks again so he couldn't see or hear her, that he was even considering changing roles and company.

Sophie's blood boiled. She was so angry at Barry for doing this to her. Angry at herself for not reporting it sooner. Angry that someone thought this behaviour was acceptable.

As soon as Jonathan arrived in the office, Sophie asked to speak to him privately.

This time, Sophie didn't hold back and told him every detail of the 18 months of harassment.

Jonathan was beyond shocked! He did a wellbeing check to ensure Sophie was OK and asked whether she wanted to go home for the day.

Then he simply said: "I will sort it out and you will be left alone."

Sophie didn't opt to go home. Instead, as she returned to her desk, she watched Jonathan march straight to the CIO to escalate the harassment.

The CIO arranged a session with Sophie to check how she was, ask some questions and then offer support. All her concerns about reporting the issue, her reputation, dealing with all the stereotypical responses to a woman reporting such behaviour washed away during that meeting.

She was not treated like a fragile, over-emotional person. Rather, she was greeted by support and recognition of who she was as an individual. Both the CIO and Jonathan were true allies.

Sophie would never quite know what was said to Barry; she never (really) heard from him again. She was finally left alone, except for some direct contact on other social media channels and a couple of emails. The emails were sent to Jonathan and dealt with swiftly.

Years later, Sophie still has Barry blocked on all social media platforms.

Even after all of this, Sophie is still friendly, warm and kind but, after this event, she is now firmer with boundaries and even more cautious around the men she works with.

Advice for men attending the office Christmas party:
"Dress appropriately
Don't get too drunk
Don't be a gossip
Don't talk to your boss
Keep your trousers on around the photocopier
Don't sleep with anyone"[24]
Advice for women attending the Christmas party:
"Stay with other people, don't put yourself in the position of being worse for wear and alone, and therefore vulnerable."
"Make sure you know how you are getting home, book your transport in advance, don't allow yourself to get stranded. Organising transport at 2am with drunk colleagues is a tough job."
"Save an 'ICE' (In Case of Emergency) contact in your phone – this is a well-recognised term used by the emergency services, just in case."[25]

---

[24] Condensed list taken from:
https://www.thegentlemansjournal.com/article/office-christmas-party/.

[25] *https://www.metrohr.co.uk/news/staying-safe-at-the-christmas-party/.*

CHAPTER 22: THE CHRISTMAS PARTY

Lucy

Lucy stood in front of her wardrobe. Her clothes hangers clinked together as she sifted through a myriad of dresses, each one presenting a new conundrum. There was the little black dress, elegant but perhaps too revealing with its plunging neckline. The red sequined number sparkled enticingly but seemed too bold. The sheer lace dress was beautiful but worryingly transparent, and the silver minidress was fun but might be too short for a work event. Each garment was beautiful yet they seemed so dangerous to her.

She sighed deeply, feeling the weight of her indecision. Tonight was her company's Christmas party in London, a highly anticipated event that promised laughter, music and a chance to let loose after a year of hard work. Yet, the thought of attending filled her with a sense of dread rather than excitement.

Lucy was new to her role, only a few months in. Approaching her 30s, she was acutely aware of the need to strike a balance between looking youthful and professional. She didn't want to dress too young and risk not being taken seriously, nor too old and seem out of touch. The added pressure of not really knowing anyone at the party only amplified her concerns.

"What if I get it wrong?" she muttered to herself. The fear of judgement loomed large in her mind. What if her colleagues thought she was trying too hard or, worse, not trying hard enough? She had seen it happen before in other workplaces, in fact she'd been unwillingly involved in the past — the subject of whispered comments, the sidelong glances, the unspoken criticisms. In the corporate world, appearances could be everything.

Lucy's thoughts were interrupted by a knock on her bedroom door. It was her housemate Samantha, who peeked in with a sympathetic smile. Samantha had an innate sense of style and confidence that Lucy often envied.

"Having a fashion crisis?" Samantha asked, stepping into the room and surveying the array of dresses.

"You could say that," Lucy replied with a weak laugh. "I just don't know what to wear. I don't want to look too...anything."

Samantha nodded. "You want to look stylish but not over-the-top, festive but not gaudy, professional but not boring. It's a tightrope walk, in heels."

"Exactly," Lucy said, relieved that someone understood her predicament. "And then there's the party itself. What if I drink too much? Or laugh too loud? Or, heaven forbid, dance, and you know I love a boogie."

Samantha chuckled. "Lucy, it's a Christmas party. You're supposed to have fun."

"I know," Lucy sighed. "But it's different for us, isn't it? We're judged on so many levels. It's exhausting."

Lucy's thoughts drifted to her male colleagues. She imagined them at home, casually selecting a suit or tuxedo for the evening, their biggest worry being whether to wear a tie or not. They didn't have to fret over whether their outfit was too sexy or too conservative, too colourful or too bland. They wouldn't be scrutinised for their choices, nor would they face whispers about their behaviour at the party.

22: The Christmas party

She thought of Scott, a manager in her department, who was known for his charm and wit. Scott could show up in a standard black tuxedo, have a few drinks, dance with abandon, and everyone would laugh along with him, not at him. He would be seen as fun, not frivolous; confident, not careless.

Lucy sighed again. The unfairness of it all weighed heavily on her. Why did women have to navigate such a minefield of expectations while men could simply show up and enjoy themselves?

"OK," Samantha said decisively, breaking into Lucy's reverie. "Let's figure this out. What do you want to wear?"

Lucy considered the options once more. "I want to look nice, but I don't want to feel self-conscious all night. Maybe something classy but comfortable?"

Samantha nodded. "How about this black jumpsuit, with the green velvet blazer paired with your gold platforms? It's festive, it's elegant, and it's not AT ALL revealing."

Lucy's eyes lit up. She had forgotten about the green velvet blazer, tucked at the back of her wardrobe.

"Yes, that's perfect," she said, feeling a wave of relief.

Samantha smiled. "Great choice. Now, let's do your hair and make-up. You'll look stunning."

The party was at a swanky hotel in central London, its grand ballroom twinkling with fairy lights and festive decorations. Lucy arrived alone, feeling a mix of excitement and nervousness.

"Oh, you're not wearing a dress," Lucy heard in the background. It was one of the senior managers, Anthony. "I was looking forward to seeing all the pretty girls in dresses."

"Is he serious?" Lucy thought.

With relief, she spotted Scott, looking effortlessly dapper in his tuxedo. He greeted everyone with his usual charisma, his laughter ringing out above the hum of conversation. Lucy watched him for a moment, marvelling at how easy it seemed for him to be the life of the party.

Taking a deep breath, Lucy decided to push her worries aside. She deserved to enjoy herself, too. She grabbed a glass of champagne from a passing waiter and joined a group of her colleagues. The music was lively, the atmosphere convivial. Slowly, she began to relax, until she saw the table plan. Obviously, her attendance was only confirmed a couple of months ago, and as a result, her whole team had a table – at the other end of the room from her. She was alone, with strangers.

David

For David, the day began with a visit to Tesco. He had been to Marks and Spencer, but £200 for a suit he would probably wear only once was far too much; it was better to buy this £70 polyester one from Tesco, He also recognised that the suit wouldn't be a 'whole company expense' if he tried to put it through his limited company. He would mix it up, though. He'd wear Church's shoes, a TM Lewin shirt and a Primark tie.

Regardless of how smart he started the evening, he thought, his outfit was likely to have some form of canopy, drink or vomit spilled upon it during the evening. Christmas parties had never been something he'd enjoyed anyway – they felt too much like enforced fun.

22: The Christmas party

David recognised the need to get on with the people he worked with, he felt honoured that they'd invited him, after all consultants are usually excluded from such things. The truth of the matter was that he'd never usually choose to go out with *all* of these people, even less so sit down, eat and then dance with them.

He gulped at the thought of dancing. He was guaranteed to split his brand new suit trousers after downing shots of Tuaca right when the DJ dropped The Sugarhill Gang. David always intended not to, but if he heard Rapper's Delight, and if he'd drunk too much, he found himself two stepping, challenging people to dance-offs and declaring himself the winner – it was all so embarrassing.

David jumped out of the cab and headed for a quick Guinness in the Golden Fleece; nobody from work would be there. It was grubby – and David liked grubby. As he drank his pint, he realised he stuck out like a sore penguin-like thumb. He reflected, "I look like my drink", which made him chuckle, so he ordered another, thinking of it as Dutch courage.

On arrival at the venue, David looked at the table plan. He was delighted to see he had been placed with Ricky, Karl and James. They were joined by Lucy, Kirsten and Gill – a decent table, though David didn't know Lucy. He was looking forward to meeting someone new.

David looked at the menu. He'd need something to absorb the Guinness later, he chuckled as he observed that the starters were just what he'd expected: basil and tomato soup with bread. And with three white shirts sitting at the table and three women probably with exposed legs and arms, nobody was going to be comfortable about the food choice.

22: The Christmas party

As people trickled into the venue, David noticed a bar upstairs and ran into Ricky, Karl and James. They chatted about football, compared their ill-fitting suits and reluctantly finished their pints. Before going back downstairs, David asked about the 'new girl, Lucy', but no one seemed to know her.

Heading over to their table, David saw someone sitting alone. He realised it was the new girl. Pleasantries were exchanged and the men did their best to put Lucy at ease. She was clearly intelligent and articulate but also nervous, and looked relieved at the arrival of Kirsten and Gill. The two women ran the PA pool, and were arguably the real powerbrokers in the company. Lucy enjoyed the stories they shared across the table, some of which made her blush.

The starters came, and as they were removed, a waiter tripped and dropped a spoon and some bits of a leftover roll onto Lucy. She brushed it off, and the waiter left, apologising profusely.

It was at this point that David felt compelled to share a fact as he sipped his drink.

"Did you know that the champagne glasses we're drinking from were modelled on Marie Antoinette's breasts?"

The men looked impressed, but the ladies less so.

David spent the next hour wondering whether he'd said something wrong, thus turning himself into a gibbering mess. He was so busy thinking about it and trying to choose his words more carefully, that he said almost nothing.

It was strange how something that felt so insignificant in the moment could feel so big as the evening progressed. And that was only his point of view – imagine how the women felt!

22: The Christmas party

David chastised himself for not thinking before he spoke and for then worrying about his own feelings before others.

Lucy

As the night wore on, Lucy found herself dancing with Kirsten, Gill and a few other colleagues. The DJ played a mix of Christmas classics and latest hits, and the dance floor was packed. Lucy laughed as she twirled around, feeling the stress of the past weeks melt away.

At one point, as Lucy was taking a breather from the dance floor, David approached her with a happy, if not slightly tipsy wave.

"Hey, Lucy," he said, his voice slightly raised over the music. "I'm so sorry about earlier. Also, I'm sorry just to come out with this, but I've been meaning to ask, have we met before? You look really familiar."

Lucy tilted her head, trying to place him. "I'm not sure. Maybe at a previous job or event?"

David shrugged. "Could be. It's just one of those things, you know? Faces you can't quite place."

Lucy laughed. "Yeah, I know what you mean. It's been bugging me all night, actually."

As she danced and chatted, Lucy felt a surprising sense of ease around her new colleagues. The majority of them were charming and funny, and David's earlier faux pas about the champagne glasses seemed to have been forgotten by everyone. Lucy and her colleagues spent a good part of the night talking and laughing, and every now and then she and David would spend a moment trying to figure out where they might have met before.

"Maybe it was at a mutual friend's party?" David suggested.

"Or a work conference?" Lucy offered.

Neither of them could pinpoint it, but the shared mystery added an interesting twist to their evening.

David and Lucy

The next morning, Lucy woke up with a slight headache but a more happy feeling than the previous day. She replayed the events of the night before and realised that her worries had been largely unfounded. Yes, there had been moments of self-consciousness, but she had also had a wonderful time.

David, too, woke up feeling lighter. His initial embarrassment had faded, replaced by fond memories of laughing with everyone, and his trousers were still in one piece – much to his wife's surprise. He still couldn't figure out where he knew Lucy from, but he was glad she had joined their table; she'd fit in well at the client's company.

Reflecting on the experience, Lucy thought about the pressures women face compared to men. It wasn't just about the clothes or the party; it was a broader issue of societal expectations. Women were often held to higher standards, judged more harshly for their choices, and scrutinised more closely for their behaviour.

Yet, last night had shown her that it was possible to break free from those constraints, even if just for a few hours. She had seen her colleagues in a different light, and they had seen her as more than just a colleague.

David, too, had a moment of realisation. He understood that his anxieties and overthinking were his own worst enemies. Watching Lucy enjoy herself despite her obvious initial nerves had made him see that sometimes, letting go and having fun was more important than the fear of judgement.

As Christmas approached and Lucy prepared for another day at work, she made a vow to herself. She would try to carry the confidence and joy she had felt at the party into her everyday life. She would remind herself that it was OK to have fun, to be herself and to not always strive for perfection.

David, for his part, decided to approach the day with a new mindset. He would be more mindful of his words but also more forgiving of himself. He wanted to enjoy his work and those he worked alongside without the constant fear of making a misstep.

Arriving at the office, Lucy's colleagues greeted her with smiles and nods, and she felt a renewed sense of camaraderie. Scott waved her over to his desk, and she joined him there, feeling lighter than she had in weeks.

"Hey, Lucy," he said with a grin. "Great party last night, huh?"

"Yeah, it was," she replied, smiling back. "I had a really good time."

"Me too," Scott said. "And by the way, that green velvet blazer was a fantastic choice. Oh, and those shoes!"

Lucy blushed slightly but felt a surge of pride. "Thanks, Scott."

As she settled into her work for the day, Lucy couldn't help but reflect on the difference between her apprehension of the previous day and her eventual enjoyment of the party. It was a reminder that while societal pressures and double standards were real, they didn't have to define her experiences or limit her joy.

In the weeks that followed, Lucy noticed a subtle shift in her own attitude. She started to care a little less about the judgements of others and a little more about her own happiness. She began to speak up more in meetings, share her ideas with confidence, and even took the lead on a new project.

Her newfound confidence didn't go unnoticed. Her manager commended her for her initiative, and her colleagues seemed to respond positively to her more assertive presence. The Christmas party had been a turning point, a moment that allowed her to see herself in a new light.

David also began to see changes. He was more relaxed around his clients, more willing to engage in conversations and share his thoughts. He no longer dreaded social events, viewing them instead as opportunities to connect and enjoy himself.

Lucy felt a sense of optimism about the future, like this was a turning point for her. She knew that there would always be challenges and that societal norms wouldn't change overnight. But she also knew that she had the power to change her own perspective, to focus on what truly mattered, and to find joy in her own way.

David shared in this newfound optimism. He realised that he could navigate the social minefield of work with humour and grace, that he didn't have to be perfect to be appreciated. Though he probably should cut back on the Guinness.

As the new year dawned, both Lucy and David found themselves navigating their professional landscapes with renewed energy. Lucy, embracing the fresh start, channelled her energies into climbing the corporate ladder within her new role. Her natural charisma and newly gained confidence played a significant role in her rapid rise. Each promotion served not only as a personal victory but as proof of her dedication and capability, challenging the stereotypes that had once made her doubt her place in such a competitive industry.

Simultaneously, Lucy launched a 'Female Friday Focus' group and newsletter. This initiative quickly gained momentum within her company and beyond, providing a platform for discussions on gender equality, sharing success stories and strategising on overcoming workplace biases. The group became a pivotal part of the company culture, influencing policies and fostering a supportive network for the women in her office.

Meanwhile, David, despite the lure of potential engagement, soon recognised the misalignment between his ambitions in his field and his newfound passion for speaking and sharing his journey to starting his own consultancy company.

David and Lucy, despite their brief encounters at the company's events, never again crossed paths within the company. As David moved on to a new engagement he and Lucy's brief interactions at the Christmas party became a distant memory for them both, David's day-to-day work was evolving to championing change within his field.

For Lucy, things would take a dip into the new year, before a chat over coffee would offer a renewed sense of purpose.

"More than half of women (54%) feel they have experienced imposter syndrome, compared with just 38% of men. Those who identify as non-binary are worse affected, with 57% doubting their abilities in the workplace."[26]

[26] *https://www.personneltoday.com/hr/imposter-syndrome-prevalence-uk-research/*.

CHAPTER 23: IMPOSTER SYNDROME

Lucy

"Are you joining this call, Lucy?" Penelope bellowed over the bank of desks.

Lucy was indeed joining the call and there were still two minutes to go before it officially started. Everyone else had already joined because they feared Penelope. In fact, Lucy had heard a rumour that Penelope had made a grown man cry and quit his job on the spot.

Lucy found the floor she worked on interesting. For once, there were more women in the tech team, but with that, there was a price to pay. One female colleague had a habit of glaring at her rudely and letting doors close on her on purpose. Lucy couldn't fathom why.

Perhaps it was the culture of the industry she was in. It was high-end retail but it wasn't exactly *The Devil Wears Prada*. As she sat musing on this, Lucy heard her name.

"Shit!" Lucy thought; she hadn't been listening.

"Lucy!" Penelope said again. "As the manager for this area, do you have anything you would like to ask? You should, because I think you need to…"

Lucy switched off again. What was Penelope's problem? Maybe she knew that Lucy was suffering terribly from imposter syndrome and out of her depth in her role.

Before Lucy could answer, her line manager interjected and started to ask questions that Lucy was pretty sure were being asked for the sake of asking or because he hadn't been listening either. Penelope was so angry she looked like she was going to explode.

After the call came to an abrupt end, Lucy felt hot and sick to her stomach. She rushed to the bathroom, sat down and started to cry.

She wanted to go home. She couldn't understand why she had been hired for this role when it was clear she wasn't good enough.

It was only a few weeks ago, that she asked her all male team in Leeds to pick up a piece of work for her.

Actually, she had needed her technical subject matter expert to fix a problem, but he didn't grasp the urgency. Lucy chased and chased with emails and phone calls. When she finally came face to face with the expert, he said:

"You know what, Lucy, maybe you should keep your nose out of it. You don't know what you're doing."

It hadn't been Lucy's finest moment. She was shaking as she aggressively responded, "Well, I am your boss and you need to do what I have asked." She had tilted her head and eyeballed him. And if she remembered rightly, there may even have been a hair toss.

Back in the bathroom, Lucy was still crying, her nails digging into her hands to try to stop herself.

"Pull yourself together," Lucy said out loud. She looked down at her watch, realising it was a long time till the end of the day.

As Lucy made her way back to her desk, she saw that Nick, a work friend she regularly had coffee with.

23: Imposter syndrome

When Nick saw Lucy's face, he locked his screen and said, "Mate, let me get us some coffees."

Lucy nodded gratefully and followed Nick to the break room. As they waited for the coffee to brew, Nick gave her a sympathetic smile.

"Rough meeting?" he asked. Lucy sighed and launched into the story, explaining how Penelope had singled her out and made her feel incompetent in front of everyone.

Nick listened patiently, nodding along. "I'm sorry, that sounds really tough," he said when she finished. "But you know what? Penelope is like that with everyone. It's not a reflection on you or your abilities at all."

Lucy looked doubtful. "I just feel so out of my depth sometimes," she admitted. "Like I'm faking it and people can see right through me."

"Impostor syndrome is so common, especially for women in tech," Nick said kindly. "But no one would have hired you if they didn't believe you were qualified for the role."

Lucy gave a small smile, appreciating his pep talk. The coffee finished brewing and Nick handed her a mug.

"Don't let Penelope get to you," he said firmly. "You're kicking ass in this job. I've seen how hard you work and how quickly you pick things up. Give it some time and the confidence will come."

Lucy took a sip of coffee, feeling a little better. "Thanks, Nick," she said. "I really needed to hear that today."

With renewed energy, she followed him back to their desks. Lucy knew she could get through this rough patch at work. All she had to do was believe in herself.

"According to UNESCO's recent report, Cracking the Code: Girls' and Women's Education in Science, Technology, Engineering and Mathematics (STEM), 57 percent of graduates in Science, Technology, Engineering and Mathematics (STEM) fields across the Arab world are women, and in the UAE 61 percent of university STEM graduates are female."

"But while it appears that the future is bright, there is a long way to go. For instance ... while 9 out of 10 women would recommend a role in tech to family and friends, 2 out of 5 have experienced some form of discrimination in the workplace."[27]

---

[27] *https://wired.me/culture/the-women-in-mena-tech-survey/*.

CHAPTER 24: CULTURAL DIFFERENCES

Sophie

Sophie stood by the window of her sleek office, her gaze lost in the sprawling cityscape below, the setting sun casting a warm glow that seemed to ignite her thoughts. Her recent offer to lead a new project in the Middle East was both an opportunity and a challenge – she needed to figure out how or if she wanted to take this chance to break new ground and face old fears. Despite her success, the thought of navigating a male-dominated industry in a culturally complex region brought back memories of her early struggles with male misogyny and unwelcome action. It was time to seek guidance, and there was no one better than Steph, whose journey through similar challenges had always inspired Sophie.

Steph, now a successful master of science graduate and keen community builder, had not only survived but thrived in the security industry in Kuwait. Her experiences, filled with trials and triumphs, made her the perfect ally for Sophie. As Sophie dialled Steph's number, her heart pounded with a mix of excitement and anxiety.

Steph: "Hello?"

Sophie: "Steph, it's Sophie. I hope it's a good time to talk?"

Steph: "Sophie! Always a pleasure. What's on your mind?"

Sophie: "I've been offered a role to run a new project in the Middle East. It's a huge step, and honestly, I'm a bit overwhelmed."

Steph: "That sounds fantastic, but I understand the nerves. It's not just a new engagement; it's a whole new world. How can I help?"

Sophie explained her concerns about cultural barriers, splitting her time between home and travelling abroad for the project, and the biases she might face. Steph listened intently, her own memories of Kuwait flooding back – the challenges of being a woman in a different culture, the changes she had to make, and the allies she found.

Steph: "Sophie, first, remember why they chose you for this role. Your skills, your leadership, and yes, your ability to adapt. You're capable of more than you think."

Sophie: "I appreciate that, Steph. But how did you manage to stay true to yourself yet respect the local culture? How did you handle this day to day?"

Steph: "It wasn't easy. But adapting doesn't mean changing who you are, you can still be bold, brave and authentic. It means understanding and navigating the environment without losing your essence. I found allies, learned the language of respect in the culture, and gradually, I changed some perceptions – and I did so whilst splitting my time between home and the region."

Sophie absorbed every word, her resolve strengthening. She knew the road ahead would be tough, but with Steph's insights, it seemed more navigable.

Sophie: "What about creating an inclusive space? I want to ensure our policies are fair and empower everyone, especially women."

Steph: "Start by setting the tone from the top. Your actions, your policies and who you hire will set a precedent. Build a diverse team, include local talents where you can, and provide training on gender sensitivity and cultural awareness."

Their conversation moved to strategies for building an inclusive workplace, from recruitment to training and everyday interactions. Sophie took meticulous notes, her vision for the project and this new branch crystallising with each piece of advice.

Steph: "And Sophie, build a support network, a community. Find local organisations that advocate for women's rights and connect with other expats. You're not alone."

Sophie: "Thanks, Steph. I guess it's about being an ally as much as finding allies, right?"

Steph: "Exactly. And remember, every small step you take sets the path for those who will follow."

Sophie: "Thanks Steph, your words have inspired me, I'm planning on being bold, brave and my authentic self."

As the call ended, Sophie felt a surge of gratitude and determination. She was not just taking on a new engagement; she was setting a precedent and creating a space where equality wasn't just a goal, but a foundational principle. And, if Steph was the example to follow, she could do so by splitting her time and location.

In the following weeks, Sophie worked tirelessly. She reached out to Non-Governmental Organisations (NGO) speaking to people in tune with the local social conditions and challenges, she hired a diverse team that included experts like Matthew, a seasoned operations lead; Zoe, a human resources leader with a passion for diversity and inclusion;

and Georgina, a fantastic advocate for equality and a sensational technology leader.

As Sophie's vision for the Middle East project began to take shape, she found herself deeply invested in assembling a team that not only brought diverse skills to the table but also represented the values she intended to champion. Together, Sophie and her team crafted job descriptions that emphasised power skills[28] over gender, revamped training programmes and introduced initiatives that celebrated cultural diversity. The UK's office walls were adorned with artwork from Middle Eastern artists, and the cafeteria menu featured a mix of their traditional cuisines.

Among the new hires was Matthew, who Sophie appointed as her operations manager. Matthew came with an impeccable track record, having overseen several successful projects in Europe. His insight into IT and operational strategies made him an invaluable asset to Sophie's leadership team. However, Matthew's appointment brought with it a unique set of challenges and concerns.

Matthew was openly homosexual, a fact that he had never needed to hide or feel uncomfortable about in his previous roles. Yet, the prospect of travelling to a region with stringent laws against homosexuality was daunting. His fears for his personal safety and well-being were real and something Sophie could not overlook. It was crucial for her to ensure not only the success of the overseas branch but also the safety and comfort of her team members.

On a return trip to London, Sophie invited Matthew to discuss the new role and address any concerns he might have.

---

[28] *https://toggl.com/blog/power-skills*.

24: Cultural differences

As they sat across from each other, the seriousness of the conversation weighed heavily in the room.

"Matthew, I want you to know how thrilled I am to have you on board," Sophie started. "Your expertise is exactly what we need to make this initiative a success. However, I understand there are personal concerns, and I want to address these head-on."

"Thank you, Sophie," Matthew responded. "I'm genuinely excited about the role and what we're trying to build. But yes, I do have some reservations about travelling to the Middle East, given my sexual orientation. It's not just a professional transition; it's a personal risk as well."

Sophie listened, nodding. She had been laying the groundwork for Matthew's arrival at the company. "I completely understand your concerns, Matthew," she said. "And I want to assure you that your safety and comfort are my top priorities. We're working closely with a local legal consultant to understand all cultural and legal implications and to ensure we navigate this landscape smartly and sensitively."

Matthew looked relieved. "I appreciate that, Sophie. I also worry about the day-to-day – how to interact, who to trust. It's a lot to consider."

"Absolutely," agreed Sophie. "Here's what we're implementing: First, we will set up clear and robust policies to safeguard our employees' rights and well-being, regardless of their background or identity. We're also considering a buddy system, where you and other expats can support each other. Plus, we will offer cultural sensitivity training for all employees, to foster an environment of respect and understanding."

Matthew felt reassured, grateful for the proactive steps Sophie was proposing.

"Moreover," continued Sophie, "we're setting up anonymous feedback channels where any concerns can be voiced safely. And I'll be there, Matthew. You won't be going through this transition alone. We'll navigate this together."

As Matthew got up to leave, Sophie felt a renewed sense of responsibility. She was not only challenging business norms but also broader societal issues, and in doing so Sophie and her team were taking on board and embracing local cultures and sensitivities. This wasn't just about opening an office; it was about opening minds, not just the locals but those of Sophie and her team. It was equally important that she and her team did not offend local sensibilities.

"We'll make sure this programme of work is a beacon of inclusivity," she assured Matthew. "Let's showcase how respect and diversity are not just Western values but universal ones."

As the project came to a close, the impact of Sophie's efforts was palpable. The team felt valued and motivated, and the local community began to see the branch as a model of inclusivity and respect.

As the new branch opened its doors, Sophie was delighted to see members of the local community coming to celebrate. One man, Ahmed, approached Sophie with a warm smile. "I wanted to thank you for the care and respect you have shown our community," he said. "It would have been easy for an outsider to come in and impose their own cultural values. But you made the effort to understand us, to learn our values, and to find common ground. What you have done here is brave –

you challenged norms not just in business but in society. By embracing diversity as a strength, you are setting an example for others to follow."

Ahmed grasped Sophie's hands in a gesture of gratitude. "Stay true to who you are," he told her. "Your open mind and open heart are what make you a leader. I applaud your authenticity and courage. You have sown the seeds for change in our community. We will watch your company grow here with hope."

Sophie was moved by his words. She had faced many challenges bringing the project to life, but in this moment, she knew it had all been worth it. With misty eyes, she thanked Ahmed for his faith in her. As she looked around at the smiling faces, her team, men and women from the community, people of different backgrounds united, she felt confident this was just the beginning. There was still much work to be done, but standing there, Sophie felt proud of what she had achieved so far. She was ready to continue on this journey of opening doors, opening minds and bringing people together through the simple act of embracing each person's humanity.

Sophie often thought back to her conversation with Steph, grateful for the guidance that helped her navigate her journey. Sophie had not only accepted the challenge but had also transformed it into an opportunity to empower, inspire and lead by example. In the heart of the Middle East, Sophie was not just a leader; she was an ally, a mentor and a catalyst for change, all whilst being her authentic self.

"The idea is that women who have climbed to senior roles could then mentor more junior men within their organization. Through this, they could help to share leadership behaviours that are non-gender specific, all the while giving the men the opportunity to work with senior women, learning about their working style and even the kind of barriers women face at work."[29]

---

[29] https://www.forbes.com/sites/adigaskell/2021/02/18/workplace-equality-improves-when-women-mentor-men/.

CHAPTER 25: SHE HELPS HIM

Lucy

"Toto, I've a feeling we're not in Kansas anymore."[30]

Lucy had taken a job in Service Management in Worthing, West Sussex, which meant she moved not just jobs, but her entire life.

Driving to her new office felt alien. Thank goodness she had passed her driving test at 17 and panic bought her £200 car to get by. As she sat in the car park waiting to go in, she looked around and instantly regretted leaving her job at the bank. But she quickly reminded herself how unhappy she had been there.

Settling in to the new job, everything felt a little old fashioned. Well, compared to the Molton Brown hand soap in the marbled bathrooms and suit and ties she was used to seeing in London. Being in the office was not a pleasant experience, from the uncomfortable chairs to the permanent smell of blocked toilets. There was no expensive Molton Brown hand soap at this company!

It was here that Lucy met John. He was working on the service desk.

The first thing he said to her was, "This is where the magic happens."

John was slightly nervous around Lucy. She was well-spoken and had an air of sophistication about her. He

---

[30] The Wizard of Oz, (1939).

wondered what she was doing there when she could have stayed at her high-powered job in London.

After her successful initiation of Female Friday Focus groups in her previous company, Lucy had found herself increasingly drawn to the role of a mentor. This initiative had sparked not only professional growth for many of her female colleagues but also a profound personal transformation within Lucy herself. She realised that her true passion lay in empowering others, a realisation that came into clearer focus with John's story.

Lucy liked John. She thought he was funny, professional and somewhat wasted on the service desk. He embodied what she felt a service professional should be: technically adept, with great customer skills and an eagerness to learn. John was a colleague who embodied the potential that could flourish under the right guidance. Lucy saw in him a burgeoning leader who needed to break beyond the confines of his current role.

"I don't think I want to stay working here," John confessed to Lucy after they had been friends for a while. Lucy empathised deeply, feeling a similar restlessness herself.

"I get it. I don't think I'll stay here either," Lucy replied. "Do you want me to take a look at your CV? Would you also like me to mentor you as well?" She knew she could contribute to John's career advancement. He didn't have her experience in changing jobs, and with a few tweaks to his CV, she felt he would be snapped up.

"Yes, please," John said.

Lucy's help proved invaluable. With her input, John's CV was transformed into a compelling narrative of his skills and potential, paving the way for his eventual departure to another company. They had also set some time aside to practice interview skills from how to answer questions to what to ask the interviewer. Lucy also helped John think about his own next steps, what that looked like, focusing on his aspirations to become a 'head of IT.'

Six months later, Lucy had since moved on. She was reminded of John one morning when a message from him popped up on her phone:

> **I just wanted to say thank you. I would never have gotten this job without your help. I have increased my salary by 30K and I wouldn't have done it without you.**

Lucy read the text and smiled. She was pleased for John as she really believed in him. If she was able to help him change his life, then her work mentoring him was almost done.

Lucy mulled over John's message, gazing out of the window of her home office, remembering London's shimmering skyline. Earlier that day, she had been reading *Wired* and was especially drawn to the stories of London's Silicon Roundabout, now known as the epicentre of London's tech scene, where innovation met ambition – a perfect backdrop for someone as driven as Lucy.

John's journey, facilitated by her mentorship, had not only elevated his career but also reinvigorated Lucy's. Her mentorship along with her success with Female Friday Focus had been pivotal experiences, proving how targeted allyship could propel individuals to new heights. Now, in her new role, Lucy was determined to leverage her experiences to make a broader impact, with half an eye on the prestigious and dynamic environment of London's technology sector.

With this in mind, Lucy proposed a comprehensive mentorship programme within her new company, designed to identify and develop potential across all levels of the organisation. Drawing on the principles that had made Female Friday Focus so effective, she aimed to create an inclusive platform that would cater not only to women but to all underrepresented groups within the tech community.

The programme combined structured mentorship with informal networking opportunities, creating a blend of support that was both professional and personal. Workshops focused on skills development, while panel discussions tackled the challenges of navigating a career in a high-pressure environment. Lucy's initiative quickly garnered attention, establishing her as a forward-thinking leader in her company.

Meanwhile, John flourished in his new role, his salary boost a testament to the tangible benefits of Lucy's mentorship. Although their paths had diverged, the impact of their brief collaboration lingered. Inspired by Lucy's guidance, John became an advocate for mentorship in his new workplace, echoing the principles he had learned from Lucy.

Lucy's continued success both in her day-to-day work and Female Friday Focus had sparked more than just career growth – it ignited a vision of how the workplace could look. The initiative had become a transformative platform under Lucy's guidance, providing support and empowerment to women within the organisation and fostering an environment where mentorship and advocacy opened doors that once seemed firmly closed.

25: She helps him

The ripples of Lucy's efforts were reaching far and wide. The acclaim of the Female Friday Focus program began to echo throughout the tech community, drawing attention from influential circles within London's technology sector. Conversations at conferences, mentions in industry newsletters and social media buzz brought Lucy's achievements into the spotlight, showcasing her as a thought leader in diversity and inclusion.

As these opportunities unfolded, Lucy felt both exhilarated and daunted. She was acutely aware of the potential these new platforms held, not just for her career but for expanding her impact on a larger scale. Each invitation to speak, each request for interviews and each discussion about potential collaborations nudged her ever closer to the heart of London's tech innovation zone.

Though she cherished her current role, Lucy knew that the burgeoning interest carried promises of new challenges and broader horizons. The success of Female Friday Focus had laid a foundation, and now the tech community was offering her a stage upon which she could further her advocacy and perhaps even shape policy and practices on a grander scale.

As the year drew to a close, Lucy found herself at a crossroads. The recognition of her work was flattering and deeply validating, yet it also posed a question of where she wanted her journey to lead next. With each conference she attended and each networking event where she represented her initiative, Lucy realised that her aspirations were growing in tandem with her reputation. She also noticed behaviours from others that both interested and annoyed her.

She began to envision a future where she could merge her passion for mentorship with her day- to-day career. Lucy felt she could use her experience to influence a wider audience, advocate for systemic change, and perhaps most importantly, mentor a new generation of tech professionals from diverse backgrounds.

The decision to add mentor to her career became somewhat of a strategic move. Lucy planned meticulously, ensuring that Female Friday Focus was left in capable hands while setting the stage to add to her career. Her goal was clear: to take what she had learned and achieved and amplify it within the larger tech community, mentoring and helping others where the impact could be even more profound.

As she learned new skills as a mentor, Lucy's days were filled with preparations and planning. She reached out to contacts, joined women in tech-focused diversity panels, and collaborated on projects that aligned with her mission. Each step was taken with a blend of excitement and resolve, driven by the knowledge that her journey was about more than personal success.

Lucy had a bigger mission.

"Women leave their positions at a far higher rate than men, and more often than not, are then replaced... by men. On average, we're looking at attrition rates of 31% vs 24%, and it only goes higher as you move up the corporate ladder. By the time you actually reach the C-suite, women leave their jobs at over three times *the rate of their male colleagues: 24% vs 7%, according to the Network for Executive Women."[31]*

[31] *https://wired.me/culture/the-women-in-mena-tech-survey/.*

CHAPTER 26: I WANT TO QUIT

Lyra

Waiting in the reception for her interview, Lyra felt good. Confident even. This job was her next move, and she was ready for it. She liked her outfit, her skin was smooth and her hair shiny. She sat up tall.

When Lyra walked into the meeting room, she realised she had already seen her interviewer a few minutes earlier – a very tall man who had passed her on the pavement. She couldn't help noticing how handsome he was, and he, for his part, didn't take his eyes off her. Lyra knew that working with this man could spell trouble for her career and potentially her reputation, but she tried hard to give the best interview she could. A few days later, she got the call offering her the job and an impressive salary. Despite her reservations, she accepted.

"Is it wrong to fancy your boss?" Lyra asked her friend Lucy over dinner one night after a few weeks in her new role.

"It depends," Lucy responded, knowing Lyra well.

"On…?"

Lucy took a sip of her drink. She paused while she considered how to phrase her answer so as not to offend Lyra but also ensure that her response embodied her values.

"If you want to progress in your career and prepare yourself for your next big role, then I would push those feelings to one side. But equally, you know me. I am sucker for love, and if this boss, Will, is, you know, the one…then I don't know what to say because I don't know what I would do."

Lyra knew what Lucy meant and knew what she had to do. She mustn't flirt or encourage Will to make an advance, and she mustn't get too attached to him. If she was in a relationship, maybe she wouldn't even be considering this. But there was something about him that she couldn't shift. He was older, he was slightly damaged and he had big aspirations. And he paid real attention to Lyra as if he saw something special in her.

As time went on, the feelings continued to bubble. Lyra and Will would go for coffee for their one-to-one meetings and would chat as if it were a date. After too many drinks one evening at the pub, Lyra confessed she was bored of being single and needed to move apartments due the rent going up at her current place – followed by how easy it would be if she had someone else to split the costs. Will, like a shot, offered his spare room if she ever needed it.

"I think we have a bit of a thing," Lyra had said.

"Oh, yes – we certainly have a thing," he had replied.

Lyra knew she was treading on thin ice.

Over the course of a few months, the honeymoon period started to fade away and the flirting fizzled out. Lyra wasn't enjoying the role anymore and Will started to get annoyed with her. Lyra didn't know what had happened, but things had dramatically changed.

"I've clearly hired the wrong person," Will snarled at her during a one-to-one. The look of endearment had faded from his eyes. His olive skin was now red as small beads of sweat formed on his brow.

Lyra was horrified. How had it come to this? Every piece of work she now did, he changed. Everything she said was apparently wrong. He made her feel small, inadequate and alone. Her team all seemed to be against her, apart from her two direct reports, who stood up for her, seeing how unfair Will was being.

In her next one-to-one, Lyra began to say it would be best for her to leave the business when Will cut her off: "If you want to quit, then quit. I can sort this out with immediate effect. It's not like you do much anyway – all you do is play dress-up."

Lyra took a deep breath and said that she wanted to negotiate an exit date. She didn't want to leave without something else to go to. Will calmed down, and agreed to a plan with Lyra.

Then the day came when she had to do her handover...

Will stood over her shoulder. Being 6ft 3, he towered over Lyra, who was sitting in her seat. She felt relieved that she had asked her colleague Pete to be in the room with her.

"Can you sit down?" she asked Will, her voice shaking. "You're significantly taller than me and you're making me feel uncomfortable."

Wills face softened. She hadn't seen that face for a while. He looked hurt. Lyra immediately felt bad, though her inner voice reminded her that as much as she used to be falling for him, he had become a bully. This internal monologue wasn't new – it had been happening from the moment she had met him. And he knew this.

"What Lyra has done as a handover is second to none," said Pete. "She really has gone into great depth and delivered what she promised."

26: I want to quit

Lyra was grateful for Pete's words. She felt safer with him there, even though it wouldn't stop Will making her feeling small for one last time.

Lyra also knew she wasn't an innocent party in this situation, taking on this job there was this risk. She had felt it in her gut. Yes, she fancied Will and yes she would flirt with him. But as soon as he realised that she wasn't going to jeopardise her career or her reputation, his attitude towards her changed. She knew that in future she needed to trust her instincts as she never wanted to be in this situation again.

"Nearly half (46%) of women in the tech industry report feeling burned out, compared to 39% of male tech professionals, according to Yerbo. This gap is not surprising given that women face many uphill battles in the IT industry, encountering obstacles that their male counterparts typically will not face in their careers."[32]

---

[32] https://www.cio.com/article/657960/burnout-an-it-epidemic-in-the-making.html.

CHAPTER 27: ALWAYS ON; ALWAYS ANXIOUS

Lucy

The Covid bubble had burst and Lucy had been asked to go back to working in the office three days a week. Alongside this, she was developing her mentoring skills. She didn't mind the work – in fact she loved it – but the three hours of commuting were seriously impacting her day-to-day life, not to mention the on-call rota that had recently been introduced.

Lucy found herself back in London, during a digital age that meant things were constantly changing. Lucy and her highly skilled team – Tom, Mia and Sam – struggled to balance the relentless demands of work with their personal lives. They were at the forefront of innovation but as a result, they were always 'on', their lives unfolding in three-week rota cycles, each with its own rhythms of urgency and quiet.

Tom, whom Lucy had appointed as mid-level manager, had his life meticulously organised around the rota. The first week was always the hardest – his team were on call and emergencies are frequent. Tom's phone was a relentless distraction, presenting a maze of urgent emails and late-night crises. By the second week, the pace slowed slightly, allowing him some respite to focus on strategic planning and long-term projects. The third week, however, Tom dedicated to recovery and preparation, knowing the cycle was about to begin again.

Despite his best efforts to stay ahead, Tom felt trapped in a continuous loop. His attempts to introduce regular, planned downtime clashed with the unpredictable nature of on-call weeks. The blurred lines between work and life eroded his sense of control, leaving him perpetually on edge.

For Mia – a software developer – the on-call rota was a non-stop juggling act. Her first week aligned with Tom's, when she was tethered to her phone, ready to troubleshoot and solve issues at a moment's notice. The week often meant sleepless nights and hurried mornings. The second week offered a slight reprieve, allowing her to catch up on personal commitments and spend time with her partner and their dog, Scooby. By the third week, she focused on self-care, trying to recharge before the cycle restarted.

Mia's challenges were compounded by her responsibilities at home. Each on-call week tested her ability to be present for her partner and his health conditions, often leaving her guilt-ridden and exhausted. She dreamed of a more flexible schedule, one that respected her dual roles as a partner, carer and tech expert.

Sam, once part of the marketing team, had transitioned into a role that suited their independent spirit better – a style guru and branding consultant. With a keen eye for design and a unique aesthetic, Sam had become a sought-after expert in corporate branding, helping companies craft their visual and stylistic identities. Despite their success, Sam struggled with the demands of being always available to clients, their creative energies often stifled by the constant pressure to perform.

Sam's approach to the rota was as stylish as their wardrobe – handled with flair but also a hint of frustration. Their weeks were spent juggling client meetings, photoshoots and last-minute design emergencies, all while trying to maintain a personal life that reflected their vibrant spirit.

27: Always on; always anxious

One late Friday afternoon, as the three found themselves together in the company's communal lounge, their conversation turned from casual complaints about the rota to a serious discussion about its impact on their lives.

"It's like being in a race where you can't see the finish line," said Tom. "Just when you think you can take a breath, another sprint starts. Nobody ever calls you to ask if you're OK. It's always 'I want this', 'this is broken', 'this is urgent'. I mean, is it REALLY?"

"Exactly," Mia chimed in. "And every sprint or call feels like it's taking a bit more out of me. There's no time to just be myself."

"Every creative spark I have needs to be saved for emergencies," agreed Sam. "It's exhausting."

Spurred by their shared frustrations, they proposed a new approach to management – a more flexible on-call schedule that included time off after particularly draining weeks and a rotation that accounted for personal circumstances.

In a meeting room looking out at the glinting Shard, Tom, Mia and Sam gathered around a large table, looking slightly anxious but determined. They were going to present their proposed new schedule to Lucy.

Always keen on fostering a supportive work environment, Lucy welcomed the discussion, her expression one of open curiosity and concern. "All right," she said as the team assembled. "This is such an important topic. Let's hear what you've come up with."

Tom, taking the lead, laid out the issue with clarity and precision.

Mia then explained the new schedule idea, outlining the buffer periods where the previous on-call team could completely disconnect before the next cycle.

Sam added a creative touch, suggesting a 'light-duty' week for team members coming off an on-call week. During this period, they could work on less demanding projects, allowing them to ease back into the full swing of things.

Lucy listened and took notes. She appreciated their initiative and was impressed by the thoughtfulness of their proposal. Sympathetic to the challenges they faced, she was also keenly aware of the need to maintain the high service levels and response times that their clients expected.

"I see the value in what you're proposing," Lucy said. "Let me think through the logistics and implications to ensure we can maintain our commitments without burning out our team. I want to support you all in a way that also sustains our business objectives."

Lucy spent the next few days consulting with Zoe in HR and other department heads, exploring the feasibility of the proposed changes. She looked into various scheduling software that could accommodate more complex rotas and reached out to other leaders in the industry for insights. Her efforts were thorough, aiming not only to address the immediate concerns of her team but to set a precedent that might benefit other departments as well.

A week later, Lucy called another meeting with Tom, Mia and Sam. She presented a revised version of their proposal, incorporating their ideas but adjusted to ensure seamless client support.

"Here's what we can do," Lucy told them. "We'll trial the new on-call rota you've proposed for three months. During this period, we'll include buffer periods as you suggested, and we'll introduce 'light-duty' weeks, but with a slight modification – these will be optional, based on individual needs and workloads."

She continued, "I've spoken with IT about setting up alerts and notifications that better respect out-of-hours time, and Zoe from HR is on board to offer additional support in the form of mental health resources and flexible working arrangements for those who've had a particularly challenging on-call week."

Tom, Mia and Sam were visibly relieved and grateful. They felt heard and valued.

"Yes, thank you," said Mia. "It feels good to know that our well-being is as important as our output."

Lucy smiled, pleased with the outcome but more so with the spirit of collaboration that had characterised the entire process. She was confident that this new approach would not only improve team morale but also enhance productivity and creativity, ultimately benefiting the company's bottom line.

"Your feedback will be crucial on this," Lucy said. "Let's make this work for everyone."

As Tom, Mia and Sam left the meeting, they exchanged smiles at the thought of a more balanced life. Lucy's leadership had turned a potential crisis into an opportunity for innovation and growth, setting a standard for how modern workplaces could adapt to the realities of their employees' situations.

There was a palpable sense of anticipation mixed with slight scepticism during the initial weeks of the new rota as everyone adjusted to the system – testing the boundaries of the buffer periods and adapting to the optional light-duty weeks. The changes, thoughtfully crafted and implemented, began to show their effectiveness gradually.

In the first month, the team experienced the benefits of having guaranteed downtime after intense on-call periods. Tom found himself enjoying uninterrupted weekends for the first time in years. He began to engage more in his hobbies and spent more time with his family, noticing a significant decrease in his stress levels.

Mia, too, felt a change. The buffer periods allowed her to plan better for her time with her partner, meaning she was more present and engaged at home. She no longer had to excuse herself from dinner to take a call or solve a crisis. This newfound predictability in her schedule brought a sense of calm to her previously chaotic life.

Sam relished the light-duty weeks, using them to explore creative projects that had been on hold. These weeks not only provided a respite from the high stakes of on-call duties but also allowed Sam to contribute in ways that fuelled their passion and professional satisfaction.

Despite these improvements, the trio couldn't shake off a level of anxiety brought on by years of being on call. The sound of a phone ringing still sent a jolt of adrenaline through them, a Pavlovian response that wasn't easy to quell. This reaction was especially pronounced when they were approaching the end of their buffer periods, at the anticipation of re-entering the on-call rota.

Tom confessed in one of their follow-up meetings, "I'm feeling so much better, but every time my phone rings, I'm bracing myself for something urgent, even on my days off."

27: *Always on; always anxious*

Mia and Sam nodded in agreement, sharing similar experiences. This ongoing anxiety was not something they had anticipated when proposing the new system, and it was clear that while the physical demands of being on call had been addressed, the psychological impacts were lingering.

Lucy recognised this and decided to bring in a psychologist specialising in occupational stress to conduct workshops for the team. These sessions focused on techniques for managing stress responses and included training on how to mentally 'disconnect' from work pressures during off hours.

The psychologist explained, "Your reactions are completely normal given your past experiences. It's a form of mild PTSD, where your body and mind are still on high alert. With time and practice, we can retrain your responses to be more in line with your current reality."

Over the remaining months of the trial period, the team practised the techniques they had learned, slowly noticing a decrease in their anxiety levels. They worked together, supporting each other when having difficulty in disconnecting or transitioning back to on-call duties.

By the end of the three-month trial, the improvements were undeniable. Productivity was up, burnout rates were down, and the overall morale had improved significantly. However, the journey to complete psychological adjustment was ongoing. Lucy committed to making the workshops a regular part of workplace training and continued to refine the on-call system based on feedback.

When the trial period formalised into a permanent schedule, Tom, Mia and Sam felt a renewed sense of control over their professional and personal lives. The fear of the ringing phone hadn't completely disappeared, but it no longer ruled their lives. They had tools and support to manage their reactions, and they had each other – a team united not just by work, but by a shared experience and a collective overcoming of one of the modern workplace's most pressing challenges.

"If you're not feeling like an imposter then you're probably in your comfort zone and that's not where the good things happen."[33]

[33] https://www.linkedin.com/posts/stevenbartlett-123_i-have-always-viewed-imposter-syndrome-as-activity-7054423031514808321-wMvr/.

CHAPTER 28: CAN ANYONE HELP?

David

David sat alone. It had gone dark, winter was setting in, the dog needed a walk, and he was about to join another meeting that didn't pay the bills.

It was one of those late evenings where the weight of his responsibilities felt like a tangible mass in the room. Mentoring women was a role David had voluntarily taken up, fuelled by memories of his mother – a woman lost to her addictions and unable to live out her true potential. That memory was both a motivator and a heavy anchor.

While David had committed himself to being an ally, a voice for those who were sometimes voiceless and a mentor to those climbing the corporate ladder, his own self-doubts often clawed at him. He knew it was imposter syndrome – the nagging belief that he didn't belong where he was, that he was a fraud, and that he would eventually be found out. Though he'd had a robust career, consulted on major IT programs and spoken at industry conferences, he wondered whether he was truly good enough.

David often found himself questioning his role as a mentor. "Am I qualified to be doing this?" he'd think, staring at his professional certifications and accolades neatly framed on his office wall. They represented expertise in his chosen field, not necessarily the wisdom needed to guide someone else's career, let alone navigate the minefield of gender politics in the tech industry.

His professional journey had been more like a series of fortunate events rather than a well-laid plan. He had evolved from a helpdesk analyst to an industry-recognised consultant, but was that enough? Did that make him a suitable mentor?

The driving force that quelled these doubts was his genuine desire to help – to give people the boost they might need to overcome systemic barriers, just as he wished he could have provided that for his mother. David realised that perhaps qualifications for mentorship weren't just about what you knew, but also about the empathy and insight you could offer. After all, some of the most valuable lessons in life didn't come with certificates.

So, each time he pondered whether he should offer his guidance, he'd think about his mother and all the others who could benefit from having just one person believe in them. This emotional resonance, he reasoned, was a qualification in its own right, one that could potentially make a lasting impact.

David understood that his role as a mentor wasn't to have all the answers but to help others find their own. Each time he overcame his hesitations and reached out to mentor, he found that his lived experiences, mistakes and victories often provided more value than any formal training ever could.

The rewards for David's mentorship efforts were often intangible but deeply fulfilling. For every lingering doubt or second-guess, there was a moment of pure, undiluted satisfaction that wiped it all away. These were the moments when he saw his mentees reach milestones in their careers, each in their unique way, reminding him that his guidance, however imperfect, had made a difference.

Take Vanessa, for instance. She had always dreamed of a leadership role but struggled with public speaking anxiety.

28: Can anyone help?

Through months of gentle conversation, reassuring emails and belief in one another, David and his peers helped her build up her confidence.

When Vanessa finally landed the managerial position she'd always coveted, her joyous LinkedIn post – "I did it, and I couldn't have done it without all of you!" was all the validation David needed.

Then there was Jeremy. Ambitious and multi-talented, he yearned to balance his tech career with serving in the military reserves. David advised him on time management, professional growth and navigating the complexities of this dual path. He prepared him for his manager saying 'no' but was delighted when Jeremy received the opposite response. The day Jeremy donned his reserves uniform for the first time, he sent David a photo with a simple caption: "Made it. Thanks, mentor."

Lyra, on the other hand, was a natural-born star who needed little but a nudge in the right direction. A guiding hand and an occasional "you've got this" were enough for her to shine brighter than David could ever dream. Lyra would go on to speak publicly, write and excel in everything she did. Seeing all this unfold made David feel like a proud parent watching a child walk for the first time. Though David sensed Lyra was still fighting an urge to leave the industry, he hoped she would find something that worked for her and gave her the creative outlet she craved.

Each of these success stories added a layer of gratification that made all the hard work and soul-searching seem trivial. These were living, breathing testaments to the fact that his mentorship had tangible value, that he was more than just a bundle of professional certifications and past regrets.

But that wasn't all. The digital world also bred imposter syndrome. Social media painted everyone, including him, as happy, successful and 'always on'. However, David knew the toll of being perpetually engaged, keeping up appearances. It nibbled at the edges of his sanity and was mentally draining. In that sense, the digital space was a double-edged sword – it provided him a platform to advocate, but also sustained a culture of constant comparison.

Adding another layer to this emotional labyrinth was David's commitment to promoting gender equality. His intentions were pure, but David was well aware of the tightrope he was walking. As a man in a position of influence, there was unspoken scrutiny, a watchful eye making sure his allyship was not another guise for the kind of casual chauvinism he had witnessed in his younger years. This made him hyper-aware of his interactions – what he said, how he said it, and the consequences that could ripple from a misplaced word or action.

His toughest battle was internal, fighting the residual guilt and sadness that stemmed from his complex relationship with his mother. He had seen first-hand what the absence of positive role models could do, how it could crush the spirit and potential of a talented individual. And while he could never go back and save his mother from herself, he found some redemption in helping others escape a similar fate.

As David finally shut down his computer and rose from his chair, he sighed. The room was dark, and the moonlight cast shadows on the walls. It was a creepy November evening. The shadows were like his inner demons, changing shape but never really going away. Yet, every day he faced them, braving the complexities and insecurities, because he knew he had important work to do.

David wanted to make the world just a little bit better than he'd found it, which he called his own tiny legacy.

"One in three women in the UK were planning to leave their tech job, according to a report by Tech Talent Charter, a tech industry group."[34]

---

[34] *https://www.computerworld.com/article/2079924/nearly-a-third-of-women-in-tech-jobs-are-considering-leaving.html#:~:text=The%20gender%20gap%20issue%20is, accounting%20for%20230%2C000%20tech%20employees.*

CHAPTER 29: ENOUGH IS ENOUGH

Lyra

It is fair to say that Lyra's time in the unforgiving world of tech had been a constant battle against ingrained sexism, misogyny and mansplaining.

After years of tirelessly fighting for her place in the industry and making a success of her career, Lyra grew tired. It killed her to admit it, but she was broken. No amount of encouragement could help her.

She decided that enough was enough.

For Lyra, this decision wasn't as tough as some might have thought. Her London dream had been destroyed, so she had packed her bags, which actually wasn't a lot, and was leaving.

Lyra left her rented cityscape apartment and moved to the golden sands of Salcombe, Devon. Perfect for her and her poodle, but also perfect for perhaps a future partner and children. Lyra had visited Salcombe before with her friend Lucy, when they both just needed a break from urban life. Lucy also had a dog too and it was a weekend filled with bottomless brunches and paddles in the ocean. One morning, Lyra walked into town to get some coffees... as she did, she knew she would be back one day. Salcombe felt like home.

Lyra had a secret ambition. Okay, maybe she alluded to it one drunken night with Lucy whilst on their staycation. Lyra's dream was to set up her own café, serving Italian coffee in the day and Italian wine and Prosecco at night. A space that would welcome all. Including dogs of course.

29: Enough is enough

During the move to Devon, an opportunity arose where she was able to invest some of her well-earned London money into buying and building a café. The building had potential yet needed some serious TLC. A little like Lyra felt. She found contractors to help her repair the space bit by bit. Each tweak and change to the café also saw a change in Lyra.

She soon became one of the locals and her regulars would grab their spot overlooking the harbour.

Being so busy with her new life, she started to forget about her past life in the big smoke.

One day, her old colleague Matthew who had always treated her with genuine respect and kindness, walked into her café. He was just as surprised to see her as she was to see him.

To Matthew, Lyra looked different. There was colour in her face, her eyes twinkled and she was a little rounder but healthier. Matthew never got the opportunity to say his goodbyes when she left and now here was his opportunity.

As they chatted, Matthew revealed that he was inspired by Lyra's bravery to take on the system when they worked together, and that Lyra's courage had helped him with his own struggles. Matthew had gone on to create a safer and more inclusive environment for those marginalised at his workplace.

Lyra was stunned and humbled to learn that her actions had such a profound impact. For the first time, she felt validated for standing up against discrimination.

Matthew's story resonated deeply with Lyra, filling the void that had been left by years of mistreatment and struggle. The unexpected reunion with her colleague showed her that her fight had not been in vain, that her resilience had sparked a positive change in someone else's life. As she listened to Matthew's heartfelt gratitude, a sense of peace washed over Lyra, replacing the lingering bitterness and disappointment, something she had been trying to let go of.

As Matthew waved goodbye, Lyra picked up her phone and called Lucy, telling her about what had happened now in the café and then the Salcombe news of Kay, the 83-year-old who told yet another tourist to 'F off'. She ended the conversation by reminding Lucy to get back to her on dates for another staycation.

In the afternoon, one of the contractors, Joe, came in to double check his handy work. Lyra really liked Joe, he was kind, intelligent, handsome and a real gentleman. She was excited to see him and wanted to tell him about the crazy morning with Matthew when she felt a rush of excitement and butterflies. Lyra realised that she needed to be brave and finally ask Joe out on a date...

Joe also wanted to ask Lyra out, but was cautious. So, he was thrilled when Lyra asked him to come back after work to sample a batch of Prosecco. Although it wasn't really his thing, she was and he couldn't wait to see her again.

With each passing day, Lyra knew that with the decision to leave behind the world of tech was the best outcome for her. She no longer questioned her worth or doubted her abilities; instead, she embraced her own strength and resilience. As the days turned into months and months into years. Lyra and Joe moved into a house over the hills. One morning, as she sat with her cup of coffee watching the sunrise, Lyra finally felt free.

Matt Rowell · 2:13 PM

Hi David,

Hope all is well.

I have been working with Lucy for a while now and for some unknown reason she is another person that seems to enjoy all things service related (I know right two people who enjoy it, who would have thought hahahaha).

Anyway I was telling her all about you and wanted to make an introduction as Lucy is brilliant and you are the man about town when it come to service etc. Lucy has a wide ranging skillset from change and transformation to coaching and people development, but thought she could benefit from chatting to yourself. I was telling her about you service interruption story from the other day. I didn't spoil it as you can deliver that one to her(or she can buy your book).

Lucy Grimwade ACC ✵ · 3:57 PM

Thanks Matt for the intro!

Hi David, nice to e-meet you. I have pinged you a connection request and it would be great to have a virtual coffee before Christmas, if you are free.

David Barrow, CITP FBCS · 3:59 PM

Hello Lucy and Matt

Thanks so much for the introduction Matt, and great to meet you, Lucy. It sounds like you are doing some great things. I'd love to connect and have that virtual coffee.

Matt Rowell · 4:27 PM

My work here is done

CHAPTER 30: THE INTRODUCTION

David and Lucy

A mutual contact of Lucy and David, not realising they had met before, decided to put them in contact. Matt, a fellow mentor on the Women in Tech programme, popped them a message on LinkedIn.

By now, David had been a mentor for years. Yet he'd always been uncomfortable with why he did it.

Elevating himself as some kind of sensei or 'wise one' didn't sit right, and it especially didn't when it came to mentoring people other than his fellow white middle-class males.

How could he, from his privileged position, offer knowledge based on his experiences? Yes, he'd had hardship and some tough times, but he'd also commented on women's appearance and sat watching as fellow males made crude comments – hell, he'd made them himself, though never intentionally.

Simply put, he'd never been in Lucy's position.

When Lucy and David met via Teams, all those thoughts swamped David. He was worried that he'd put his foot in it.

Meanwhile, Lucy hadn't really wanted to join the meeting, assuming David would be narrow-minded and patronising. She decided that if she had to, she'd join, smile and never speak to David again.

The call began, and they introduced themselves and their backgrounds. Lucy and David both realised they'd been in the same industry a few years before.

"Wait a minute!" exclaimed Lucy. "We worked in the same place! And it's just occurred to me – I saw you in Browns running away from a dancer!"

"No way!" they said in unison.

Instantly, the mood lightened. Their paths had crossed twice in their past and here they were, about to discuss if David could mentor Lucy, indeed if Lucy needed David to mentor her!

Lucy was obviously a skilled professional and a fantastic communicator who was not afraid to discuss her positive feminist beliefs. If David was honest, this worried him.

Would she discover that this man was out of his depth? She already knew him as someone who went to strip clubs. Would she think him more of a hindrance than a help?

David's mind worked quickly, though often his mouth overtook it and put him at a disadvantage, so he told Lucy that he wasn't sure why he was doing this. He explained his insecurities about being a mentor.

Smiling, Lucy became the mentor instantly herself. "You're offering to help others; you are offering allyship," she encouraged him. "More people need to do so – it's important that men help women and that women don't judge all men in the same way."

30: The introduction

It was right here when the penny dropped, and David discovered what allyship really was.

He discovered that male mentoring and offering allyship to females could be a positive and valuable practice when done with genuine intentions to support and empower women. It was not a case of males dominating females. In fact, it could help bridge gender gaps, promote diversity and inclusion, and contribute to a more equitable workplace.

In their conversation, Lucy and David agreed that the key lay in the approach and intention behind the mentoring and allyship. It should be clearly thought out, and it *must* be an act of genuine intent. No matter what others thought.

They also laughed at how uncomfortable they both were that night in Browns.

"Studies have shown that 53 per cent of freelancers have trouble finding work, while 50 per cent have an irregular income and almost half of those who are self-employed feel less productive, depressed and anxious too." [35]

---

[35] *https://www.allbrightcollective.com/edit/articles/self-employed-anxiety*.

CHAPTER 31: SELF-EMPLOYED AND SELF-SUFFICIENT

Lucy

"Should I, and what if I regret it?" These thoughts would spin round and round in Lucy's head.

The permanent, full-time role Lucy was now in was causing her dread; she'd yearn for Fridays and gasp at how quickly Monday would come around. This turned into disliking Sundays, because it was 24 hours until working hell.

Over the last few months, these feelings had created an almost insurmountable level of anxiety; she'd be anxious that she was making it feel worse than it was and she was worried that her boss was looking at her in an inappropriate way. Or was it in her head? Was she facing a glass ceiling as a woman in the workplace or was she making it all up?

And if she left, what on earth could she do? Bills needed paying and her partner might not be happy with her decision. The stress was beginning to affect her daily interactions.

Lucy begrudgingly dialled into a call she was booked on. Her mood was dark, and this wasn't on her list of priorities. It was a mentoring session with David, though he wasn't the issue.

As Lucy and David exchanged pleasantries, there was a pause when neither spoke for fear of speaking over the other. David broke the silence. "Are you okay?" he asked.

"No," Lucy said.

Another pause. "Can I help?" David asked. "It's what we're here for."

Lucy poured her heart out. She told him about the misogyny and mansplaining at her workplace, her creation of a diversity and inclusion network, a group to support other women and minority groups, and her YouTube channel. She explained how these things were now being used against her, sighted as a 'distraction' to her day-to-day service delivery job involving services that she considered about as useful as an inflatable dartboard.

For 15 minutes Lucy shared her job issues, her desires to do something more meaningful and her worries about the mortgage, the bills, her dog and her own mental health.

As Lucy finished, David suggested she take a moment to breathe. He smiled and said, "I wish I were there to offer a hug of reassurance." In fairness, David took himself aback with that statement; he barely hugged anyone.

"Lucy," he continued, "I've never stepped in your shoes and I never will. But today, we arrive at a similar point to one I found myself in 15 years ago, when I hated my job. I dreaded Mondays so much that I was a bit awful and fractious until 12:01 on Wednesdays. This went on for five years. It was five years of great reviews, pay rises and bonuses, and then one day I saw what they charged me out for. I realised that day that behind the facade of annual reviews, salary bands and bonuses, I was just another pawn being moved around. It was the day I decided to set up my own business; I literally registered it in my lunch hour."

"That business sat there for a further year as I worried and stressed, until one day someone called me at 2 am to 'escalate' a service being unavailable; that service was a dating site for GILFS – Grandmas I like to Fu$k. It was the straw that broke the camel's back. I resigned before they held me to a six-month notice period."

"My advice: GO FOR IT. We are very similar, and I 100% know you will be super successful if you set up as Lucy Inc."

Lucy and David ran through Lucy's concerns one by one:

"Am I acting impulsively?" – No, you've felt this way for years.

"Maybe I'm just overthinking" – No, you are under thinking, about yourself, about your health, about your potential.

"What if I'M the problem?" – No, no, no – you are the solution.

"Globally, according to our analysis, more than two-thirds (69 percent) of all speakers were male, while less than one-third (31 percent) were female."[36]

[36] *https://www.bizzabo.com/blog/event-gender-diversity-study.*

241

CHAPTER 32: DID YOU GO SHOPPING?

Lucy

Lucy's confident stride echoed through the cavernous expanse of the East London conference centre, the industrial charm of the venue filled with a sea of tech enthusiasts, entrepreneurs and corporate suits.

It was the annual IT Tech Support conference, an event that attracted professionals from all corners of the tech industry to East London's revitalised docks, a place once gritty with maritime labour and wasteland now polished to urban chic. The air was thick, not just with the aroma of overpriced coffee and expo booth giveaways focused on craft beer and ball sports, a reminder of the gender dynamics still pervading the tech world.

The previous day, Lucy had taken the stage as a keynote speaker to discuss allyship in the workplace. Her session, in collaboration with David, was aimed at unravelling the complexities of support and advocacy within corporate structures, and was a resounding success. She spoke with fervour about the need for inclusivity, drawing nods and applause from a crowd that was surprisingly diverse for such a male-dominated field. After their speech, emotionally spent but satisfied, she had retreated to her hotel with her colleague Sophie, skipping the post-conference mingling to gather her thoughts and recharge.

Today, back at the venue, Lucy was here to listen, learn and network. Her badge, boldly labelled "SPEAKER", hung prominently as she navigated through the crowds. But despite her clear credentials and the insights she had offered just a day before, her presence as a professional seemed momentarily invisible when she was accosted by a sales person from a prominent tech firm.

"Sorry, I didn't see that session," Lucy said when the man asked if she'd seen his previous day's marketing event.

Lucy was taken aback by the man's assumption that she had been anywhere but the stage. "Why, did you go shopping?" he continued.

Lucy stood there, aghast, her mind grappling with the audacity of the question. Yesterday, she had been a voice of authority; today, she was being casually diminished to a shopping-spree stereotype. "No, I was decompressing after speaking on the keynote stage," she corrected him in a tone that masked her irritation.

The sales guy glanced down, his eyes landing at chest level. Lucy caught the direction of his gaze, the all-too-familiar drift that women in her field battled against tirelessly. "Excuse me, eyes up here, please," she asserted, her voice calm but firm.

Caught like a rabbit in the headlights, the man stuttered out an apology, "I am so sorry," his face flushing with embarrassment. Lucy, mastering the situation with grace, replied, "No problem; mistakes happen," and turned to leave, her dignity intact but her patience thinning.

As Lucy walked away, the rhythmic thud of a punching machine at a nearby gaming booth snapped her fully back to the moment. Seizing the opportunity for one last pointed remark, she turned back briefly and said to the still-flustered salesman, "I hope you and your mates enjoy that," a subtle nod to the immature behaviour at the gaming booth before raising an eyebrow and continuing on her way.

32: Did you go shopping?

"What was all that about?" queried Georgie, Sophie and David as they caught up with her. They had witnessed the exchange from a short distance, puzzled by the brief yet obviously charged interaction.

"You wouldn't believe me if I told you," Lucy started, her stride unwavering as they moved towards the scent of fresh coffee, the sprawling displays of new tech startups flanking their path.

"In fact, of course you would," she corrected herself, realising these people – her people – knew all too well the type of encounters she faced as they had faced them or seen them themselves.

Laughter broke among them as they passed by an impressive display featuring an F1 car, a symbol of speed and innovation, yet starkly contrasting with the slow progress in changing industry stereotypes.

As they settled down with their morning coffees, Lucy's mind revisited her own words from the keynote speech. The need for allyship, for voices that uplifted and challenged, had never felt more pressing. Inspired by the day's earlier frustrations, she resolved to expand her efforts, considering how she could use her experiences to fuel her next talks, maybe even a book on the subject.

As the lively chatter and the clinking of coffee cups filled the air, David noticed a lingering tension in Lucy's demeanour. Sensing that the earlier incident had struck a deeper chord, he gestured subtly towards a quieter corner of the conference hall.

Once secluded from the buzz of the conference, David's expression grew serious. "Lucy, are you OK? That was quite a moment earlier," he asked, his concern evident.

32: Did you go shopping?

Lucy sighed, a mixture of frustration and resolve flashing across her face. "Yeah, I'm fine. It's not the first time something like that has happened, but it really annoyed me. We talked about change and advancement yesterday, and yet here we are, still dealing with the same old stereotypes and nonsense," she admitted.

David nodded in agreement, understanding all too well the challenges she described. "Yesterday, you were inspiring, Lucy. That hasn't changed today. We'll educate him someday. It makes me think...there's so much more we could be doing to address these issues."

Lucy looked thoughtful, her earlier irritation slowly morphing into a spark of determination. "You know, David, I've been thinking about doing something more substantial about this – something that goes beyond just talking at conferences."

David's interest was piqued. "Like what?"

"Well," Lucy paused, choosing her words carefully, "do you know what, I need to think on it some more, but I think we need a platform where we can share these experiences more broadly, maybe develop some real-world solutions or guidelines that others can adopt. We could really build upon the presentation we gave yesterday."

David was inspired. "That sounds like a great idea, like a tale told from multiple perspectives. Together, we could really make an impact!"

Lucy nodded, feeling a wave of excitement wash over her. They both recognised the potential in their combined efforts.

In their silence, a shared thought lingered between them, an unspoken idea about writing a book. It was a project that could bring together their knowledge and experiences, offering a tangible resource that went beyond their industry. However, neither Lucy nor David voiced this thought just yet, each unsure of how the other would respond to such a proposal.

As they rejoined their group, the seed of their future collaboration had already been planted.

That moment of causal sexism by the salesman had unexpectedly sown the seeds of a project that might one day resonate and build on Lucy and David's mutual desire to foster change and make a lasting impact.

"By 2025, there will be just one woman for every 115 tech roles in the UK."[37]

---

[37] *https://codefirstgirls.com/blog/10-reasons-why-women-dont-apply-for-your-tech-roles/*.

CHAPTER 33: THANK YOU, NEXT

Lucy

As another rejection came through for a job that Lucy was over-qualified for, Lucy sprang into action. Over the years she had built a little black book of recruitment personnel contacts, so she picked up her phone and started dialling the different numbers. Each recruiter she spoke to, she was met with the same lines of "it's the market at the moment Lucy, it will pick up" and "you have so much experience, I don't know why you are not getting any call backs."

"Yeah, real helpful guys" Lucy sighed.

Lucy then made contact with another recruiter who she thinks she might have met in a previous role. She didn't think he was the one that Lyra had warned her about. Lucy dropped him a LinkedIn message and within a few hours they were on the phone. Brad had been in the industry for a while and had established his own agency. The call started out quite positive with the usual feedback about how the market is slow. Brad started going through Lucy's LinkedIn.

"Hmm" he said. "So, you have great experience, working on a service desk, as a service owner, service delivery manager, then suddenly you're a coach? A speaker? An author? Like, who are you? This make no sense to me, this is why people won't hire you."

Lucy sat in silence, shocked. It was contradicting advice from what she had always been told to do.

"And also, I think you are too junior to be offering consultancy." His words pierced through her ears, she felt herself cringe and her tummy was in knots.

It wasn't that she agreed with this Brad, but she certainly felt something. A mixture of "who the heck does this guy think he is?" And, "is this a sign that I have got to get out of this game?"

Lucy felt frustrated and defeated after the call with Brad, his comments left her questioning everything.

Later that day, Lucy met David for coffee. David worked in the same industry, he had also diversified and branded himself as more than 'just a consultant'. Lucy valued his advice. As they caught up over their latte and mocha, Lucy described her conversation with Brad.

"That seems really out of line," David said, shaking his head. "You have a strong CV, your LinkedIn presence is second to none and its obvious that you have plenty of relevant experience. I'm surprised he would criticise your career pivot like that, if anything it illustrates your abilities to offer so much more than just expertise in one area."

Lucy sighed, "I just don't get it. I've applied for so many roles that I'm qualified for, but I keep getting rejected. Meanwhile, you've told me about multiple offers you've turned down recently. What am I doing wrong?"

David furrowed his brow thoughtfully. "Now that I think about it, the dynamics do seem a bit strange," he said. "We have very similar backgrounds, ok, I've got a few years on you but not much else. I'm getting recruited like crazy and you're struggling. I wonder..."

His voice trailed off, but Lucy could tell they were thinking the same thing. Could it be that recruiters were favouring David simply because he was a man? The more Lucy considered it, the more plausible it seemed. She and David had the same skills and experience. The only major difference was their gender.

"Don't give up," David encouraged. "You're smart and talented. The right client will recognise that if you keep putting yourself out there." He promised to talk to some of his recruiter contacts on her behalf.

Lucy left feeling slightly better knowing she had an ally in David. But an uneasy thought lingered: if recruiters were filtering candidates based on gender, how could she ever get a fair shot? She resolved to push harder to get her skills and ideas in front of the right people. With perseverance and the support of others, Lucy hoped the tide would eventually turn.

As David and Lucy said their goodbyes and headed to their respective train's, Lucy's email pinged. It was another a rejection email.

"Thank you, next..." she said to herself.

"Eight in ten (84%) Britons think that (heterosexual) men and women can be just friends, while just 6% think they cannot, and this view is shared by both men and women."[38]

---

[38] *https://yougov.co.uk/society/articles/38505-yougov-friendship-study-part-four-friendship-and-g*.

CHAPTER 34: FRIENDSHIPS

David, Emma, Lucy, Matt

To all who met him, it seemed that David was a man who had his life together. By now, he was an author, carried out public speaking and worked as a management consultant with globally prodigious clients. He was also a loving husband to his wife of 21 years, Emma.

Meanwhile, Lucy who had just secured a role with a great client was now seen as the rising star in the technology and coaching world, known for her incredible communication skills. She was deeply committed to her relationship with her long-time boyfriend, Matt, too.

Little did David and Lucy know that their friendship was about to come under scrutiny.

It all began at a crowded networking event in the heart of London. David had been invited to speak and Lucy was a guest of honour due to her success with her "Are We There Yet?" LinkedIn newsletter questioning misogyny and sexism in the workplace. Lucy sat in the front row as David delivered his speech on the art of creating communities to act as allies to one another. She was proud as punch to see him on stage and call him a friend.

After the talk, Lucy and David moved away from the stage and chatted over a mocha and a green tea. They discussed their shared passion for effective communication.

Over the next few months, David and Lucy's professional relationship continued to grow stronger. They began collaborating on various public-speaking projects, sharing tips and honing their skills together. Their relationship was based on respect for one another's work and home lives, and an unwavering commitment to their careers.

Despite their professional synergy, rumours started to circulate. Some people couldn't help but wonder if David and Lucy were more than just friends. They were often seen attending events together, sharing jokes, which only intensified the speculation. Even their partners, Emma and Matt, occasionally had to address these unfounded rumours.

One evening, over a casual dinner with David and Lucy's respective partners, the topic of their friendship came up. Emma looked at David with a playful smirk. "You spend a lot of time with Lucy these days, don't you?"

David chuckled, reaching for Emma's hand. "Lucy is my friend. We work closely together, but it's strictly professional."

Matt chimed in, defending Lucy. "And I can vouch for Lucy's dedication to her work. She's always talking about how much she enjoys working with and learning from David."

Matt and Emma exchanged knowing glances, realising that the rumours were baseless. They trusted their partners implicitly and knew that their relationships were built on strong foundations.

David and Lucy continued to thrive in their professional relationship, collaborating on more significant projects and making a name for themselves in their respective fields. They became known as the dynamic duo of public speaking.

At one point, David and Lucy were working with the same client. While preparing for a major presentation, David and

34: Friendships

Lucy found themselves in fits of laughter over a comically awkward encounter David had had with an earlier client. Their laughter was infectious, and the entire office soon caught up with the joke. The incident became legendary within their client's workforce, and it was clear to everyone that David and Lucy's bond was unbreakable.

Back at home Emma joined David in the kitchen as they prepared an evening meal, she was amused by his recounting of the day's events. "You and Lucy seem to have way too much fun at work. I'm starting to think I should be jealous."

David grinned and reached for Emma's hand. "There's no need for jealousy, my love. Lucy and I share a friendship, but it's you who holds my heart."

Emma smiled, reassured by David's words. "I know, David. I trust you completely. Besides, Lucy is a wonderful person."

Meanwhile, Lucy was also sharing a light-hearted moment with Matt. "I swear, Matt, David has the most incredible ability to turn any situation into a comedy show. It's great to enjoy working with someone and to develop such a friendship."

Matt chuckled, wrapping his arm around Lucy. "I trust you, Lucy. Your success is a testament to your hard work, and I'm proud of everything you've achieved."

Despite the unwavering support of their partners, David and Lucy couldn't ignore the persistent rumours about the nature of their relationship. It seemed that no matter how many times they clarified their friendship, there were always doubters. They decided to tackle the issue head-on.

One evening, they hosted a joint public-speaking workshop, and during a break, David addressed the elephant in the room. "Ladies and gentlemen, we've heard the rumours. Let me be absolutely clear – Lucy and I are close friends and professional collaborators. We respect each other immensely, but there's nothing romantic between us. It's essential to dispel these misconceptions and focus on our goal of improving public-speaking skills and sharing our message that men can be allies to women and not hold some hidden agenda."

Lucy nodded in agreement. "David is not just a mentor; he's a friend who has helped me so much in my career. We should celebrate the idea that men and women can be friends, allies, and support each other."

Their candid and heartfelt message resonated with the audience, and the rumours gradually died down. People started to see David and Lucy's friendship for what it was – a genuine bond based on mutual respect and shared ambitions.

As the years passed, David and Lucy's careers continued to soar. David was regularly invited to speak at international conferences, and Lucy became a sought-after coaching guru and speaker. They continued collaborating on projects, sharing the stage and inspiring audiences worldwide.

Their successes extended beyond their careers. David and Emma built outside hustles involving art and ceramics, while Lucy and Matt decided to tie the knot and move to Malaga, Spain. David and Lucy remained close friends, celebrating each other's milestones and supporting one another through the ups and downs of life.

One evening, during a visit to Lucy in Malaga, they sat together on a rooftop terrace. Lucy reflected on their journey, "David, look at how far we've come. From a strip club to my rooftop terrace in Malaga, becoming the best of friends and allies in our careers."

David smiled warmly. "It's been an incredible journey, Lucy. I'm grateful for our friendship, and I'm proud of everything you've achieved."

Lucy leaned closer, her voice filled with sincerity. "And I'm proud of you too, David. You've been an amazing mentor, friend and ally. We've shown the world that men and women can have meaningful friendships without any hidden motives."

As they clinked their glasses together, they knew that their friendship was a testament to the power of respect, support and genuine connections between people of different genders. They had proven that men and women could indeed be friends, allies and collaborators, and that their bond was unbreakable.

In a world filled with misconceptions and stereotypes, David and Lucy's story served as a shining example of the beauty of friendship and the limitless potential that could be unlocked when people came together, regardless of their gender, to support and uplift one another.

"Today, women represent just over a quarter of current STEM workers in the UK, and there is a noticeable gap between girls and boys who study STEM subjects beyond GCSE (35% of girls versus 80% of boys). In a sign that this gap could close, the survey found that of generative AI users interested in pursuing careers or further study in STEM, 44% are women, and 56% are men."[39]

---

[39] *https://www.silicon.co.uk/e-management/skills/women-in-tech-2024-553726*.

CHAPTER 35: 2024 AND BEYOND

David and Lucy

David and Lucy found themselves on the London Underground one sweltering July afternoon, travelling home after a day of attending a conference together.

Lucy, dressed in a light and airy summer dress, gracefully walked down the platform beside David. However, the summer breeze had other plans. Just as they neared the edge of the platform, a sudden gust lifted the hem of Lucy's dress, revealing more than she or David had anticipated. Her cheeks flushed with embarrassment, but she decided to defuse the situation with humour.

With a wry smile, Lucy turned to David and quipped, "Well, I guess my dress wants to join the wind in its dance today."

David chuckled, appreciating Lucy's ability to handle the unexpected with grace and humour. "Seems like it," he replied, playfully.

But beneath the light-hearted exchange, both of them couldn't help but wonder if the other was uncomfortable. The silence that followed felt a bit awkward.

Lucy glanced at David, trying to gauge his reaction. She found him looking back at her with a warm, reassuring smile. It was as if he was silently saying, "It's OK, we're all human, and embarrassing things happen."

David, on the other hand, wondered if Lucy was genuinely OK with the situation or just putting on a brave face. He admired her ability to make light of it but didn't want her to feel uncomfortable in his presence.

As the train approached, Lucy decided to break the silence. "You know," she began, "I've had my fair share of wardrobe malfunctions, but this one takes the biscuit."

David chuckled again. "Well, it was a surprise for both of us, I guess," he replied, putting her at ease.

Their train arrived, and they stepped aboard, continuing their journey home with a newfound camaraderie. The incident brought them closer, highlighting their ability to navigate uncomfortable situations with humour and empathy.

As the train clattered along the tracks, the confined space of the carriage seemed to draw Lucy and David into a deeper conversation than they'd had at the conference. The shared laughter over Lucy's wardrobe mishap had softened the barriers that the pressure of delivering in professional settings often erect. Lucy shared her thoughts about the future, her ambitions and the project that was slowly taking shape in her mind.

David, sensing that Lucy had more on her mind, encouraged her to speak freely. "So, how did you feel about today's sessions?" he asked.

Lucy appreciated the opening. "The sessions were great, but they made me think about how much more is possible," she began. "I've been working on something – a concept really – that I believe could make a significant difference."

David leaned in, intrigued. "Tell me more," he urged.

"Well, I've been conceptualising a community platform, with the aim of supporting women in tech." Lucy paused, searching for the right words. "It's designed to support women in their careers, their lives, and help their allies too.

A space where empowerment and practical guidance meet, fostering growth and collaboration."

David was enthused. "That sounds incredible, Lucy. What inspired you to start this?"

Lucy's eyes sparkled with passion as she explained. "It's something I've been mulling over for a while. At every turn in my career, I've seen talented women struggle to find the same footholds as their male counterparts. Not to mention the countless informal conversations I've had with women who don't know where to turn for mentorship or support. I want to change that narrative."

David nodded, clearly moved by her dedication. "And you want this platform to be a catalyst for change, to help women and their allies break down barriers together?"

"Exactly," Lucy affirmed. "I envision a vibrant community where women can find mentorship, resources and advocacy. Where allies – men like you, David – can learn how to support effectively and contribute to a culture of inclusivity."

The conversation deepened as they discussed potential challenges, such as securing funding and ensuring a diverse and inclusive platform that truly addressed the needs of women across different industries, not to mention the challenges of those who misunderstood the intentions.

David offered his insights on possible strategies for engaging allies and building a supportive network around the initiative. "You know, Lucy, this could really take off with the right backing and visibility. Have you thought about partners or sponsors?"

Lucy had considered this, but discussing it with David opened new avenues of thought. "I've started to reach out to potential sponsors and even drafted a proposal for a few tech companies known for their diversity initiatives. Your feedback would be invaluable."

"I'd be honoured to help," David responded. "And Lucy, you have something special here. This isn't just a project; it's a movement. I can see it growing, influencing policies, shaping careers, changing lives."

Their train ride ended too soon, pulling into the station where they would part ways. "Let's continue this conversation soon," Lucy suggested as they walked towards the exit. "Maybe over coffee? There's so much more to plan and discuss."

David agreed wholeheartedly. "I'm looking forward to it. Let's make sure this gets the attention and structure it deserves."

Little did they know, that this idea would go on to take a slightly different direction – *actually*.

"It's not the 90's anymore. The changing face of IT leadership is shifting as new generations enter the work force. Perhaps now it is more important than ever to have power skills in IT Leadership Teams."[40]

---

[40] *https://blog.iil.com/the-benefits-of-power-skills-for-it-leaders-and-how-to-build-yours/.*

CHAPTER 36: THE POWER SKILLS

David and Lucy

The sleek, modern boardroom of the office high-rise was lined with large windows showcasing the city skyline. A large oval table occupies the centre of the room, around which Lucy and David are seated with digital tablets and notes in front of them. The room buzzes with a sense of purpose and anticipation.

"All right, everyone," Lucy started. "Let's focus on the task at hand – revising the job descriptions for our vacancies to ensure they're inclusive and reflective of the skills we value most. We want to avoid the pitfalls we've encountered in our own careers."

"Exactly," agreed Vicki, Lucy and David's new pro-bono client who they were working with to improve the organisation's job descriptions. "It's crucial that we eliminate any gender-coded language. Words like 'he' or 'she' shouldn't define our candidates."

"Let's avoid words like 'dominant' or 'competitive' which are more masculine in nature."

"Let's ensure job titles accurately describe the job. Replace creative titles with words like ninja, rock star, and superhero (gender-coded masculine words) with neutral, descriptive titles like project manager, systems engineer, trainer, or sales territory manager."

"We must also minimise the list of requirements and keep them job-related. Research shows that women are less likely to apply for a job unless they meet 100% of the requirements."[41]

"It's about creating a culture where everyone, regardless of gender, feels valued and can thrive."

"Fantastic!" Lucy said. "Speaking of thriving, we have our first round of candidates for the new roles today. Luis, Betsy and Rosy will be joining us shortly. Let's make sure we set the right tone from the start."

Moments later, Luis, Betsy and Rosy took their seats, shifting slightly nervously. However, the atmosphere was friendly and you could feel the excitement crackling in the air.

Vicki smiled warmly. "Welcome, everyone. We're excited to discuss your potential roles here. We pride ourselves on fostering an inclusive environment where power skills are as important as technical knowledge."

Luis was the first of the candidates to respond. "I've read about your initiatives and the emphasis on soft skills. I believe my experience in team leadership and conflict resolution in diverse teams would be an asset here. I love the fact that you are building something here, a community as much as a company."

Betsy joined in enthusiastically: "And I've been an advocate for mental health awareness in the workplace, which has taught me a lot about compassion and empathy in leadership. I'm eager to bring that perspective here. I'm so pleased that you've seen beyond the technical role aspects and into the

---

[41] *https://www.employerscouncil.org/resources/words-matter-gender-coded-language-in-job-ads/*.

future – a future where we can work together to deliver amazing results."

"My background is in customer service management," added Rosy. "Active listening is crucial in my current role. It's shaped my approach to all interactions – listening to understand, not just to respond. I cannot wait to work with you all and deliver on your values of providing an exceptional experience to colleagues and customers."

"Thank you all for sharing," responded Lucy. "Those are exactly the kind of skills our client Vicki values. Leadership isn't just about guiding projects but about nurturing people. It's clear that you each bring a unique set of skills that align with the company's core values. What we're looking to do next is not only assess technical abilities but also how well you integrate and elevate the company's culture through these power skills."

"This is what changing the narrative looks like," Vicki explained. "We're not just filling roles; we're strategically aligning our team for inclusive and holistic growth."

As the meeting concluded some time later, the room felt energised. Lucy and Vicki exchanged a look of satisfaction, knowing they were on the right path for them and their teams to thrive.

Lucy thought that her past could have a positive impact on everyone's future, and it was at that moment that David also observed the pride in Lucy's eyes.

Days later, David was sitting in a corner of a busy bar, his eyes glued to the screen of his smartphone as he prepared to speak at an event.

Around him, the hum of conversation blended with the clatter of glasses and the sounds of ice being mixed with cocktails. With a smile on his face, David was absorbed in another world – a world being reshaped by Lucy.

On his screen were a series of job descriptions, freshly crafted and newly posted for Lucy and David's client. As David read through the text, he could clearly see that Lucy, Vicki and he had agreed job descriptions that were revolutionary in their intent and design, obviously aimed at creating a diverse and inclusive workplace.

As David scrolled through each listing, he couldn't help but feel a mixture of pride and hope. He could see that the client had put their work into practice, these roles not only demanded technical expertise but also emphasised a commitment to diversity and inclusion to accompany their client's equal opportunities employer statement.

David sipped his Guinness – not the best, but then he was in a cocktail bar. His thoughts drifted to his own experiences in the industry. He had seen first-hand the barriers that often discouraged or side-lined talented individuals from underrepresented groups. Now, as he read through these job descriptions, he saw a clear break from the past. Here was an overt commitment to change –not just in policy but in practice.

His eyes lingered on a section highlighting the company's commitment to continual training and development, especially in areas related to diversity and cultural awareness. It was an assurance to candidates that they would be joining an organisation that not only valued their skills but also their personal growth and well-being.

David's thoughts were interrupted by a notification on his phone. It was an email from Lucy, she had also just read the job descriptions they had worked on with their client.

Lucy's message read:

> **Hello! Did you see the JD's, isn't it great when a client takes on board your advice and isn't it even better when you see the advert online, for people to apply to.**

Before David finished, up popped another bubble on the screen:

> **Let's change the world, one job description at a time.**

David immediately sent a response:

> **Totally!**

After he hit send, he finished his Guinness. Six out of ten at best. Ten out of ten was the incredible fulfilment of seeing Lucy instigate meaningful change.

David knew that the road ahead for both of them would be filled with challenges, but also immense opportunities to influence industries in profound ways.

Later in the week he was speaking about the co-creation of value and allyship, and he knew that this along with his work with Lucy, was really beginning to bear fruit.

CHAPTER 37: LET'S WRITE A BOOK

David and Lucy

David glanced at his watch, noting that it was nearly time for his scheduled call with Lucy. He adjusted himself in his seat, making sure the lighting wasn't too harsh against his background of neatly organised bookshelves now containing books he'd authored himself.

As the clock struck the hour, he clicked 'Join' and Lucy joined immediately afterwards.

"Hey, Lucy! How's everything at your end today?" David asked.

Lucy's eyes sparkled with enthusiasm as she responded from her home office, bedecked with a poster that stated "Don't be like the rest of them, darling", a stark contrast to David's more traditional setting.

"Busy as always, client work is taking off but I'm never too busy for our chats, David. What's on the agenda today?" David leaned forward, his voice tinged with excitement that hinted at something beyond their usual discussions.

"So, I've been thinking," he began, "about how much we've shared over these past months. The mentoring sessions, the career management, the wins, and the losses. We've really covered a lot of ground, haven't we?"

Lucy nodded, her curiosity piqued. "We sure have – we've had laughter, tears, frustration, and of course, the dogs. The dog conversations are the best." Right on cue, Pippa barked and Norris groaned at different ends of the call.

"Well, what if we took all these stories, all these lessons we've learned, and put them into something...bigger, like we were talking about before?"

Lucy's face lit up, realising she knew what was coming next.

David clasped his hands together. "I don't want to make you uncomfortable, or do anything you don't—"

Before he could finish, Lucy cried, "Let's write a book!"

"Yes, yes, yes!" responded David. "And not just any book, but one that captures our journey from mentor and mentee to something much closer to friends and confidantes. We can use our experiences to showcase the importance of building supportive, empowering relationships and most importantly allyship in the world of work – and beyond."

Lucy leaned back, her mind visibly racing with the possibilities. "David. I love it. We could structure it around the key moments where we really leaned on each other, turning our personal stories into a guide for others in the industry. It could be a roadmap for building effective, supportive connections."

"Exactly," David agreed enthusiastically. "We can dive deep into the nuances of our interactions. The informal coffee chats, the late-night troubleshooting sessions, the strategic wins, that 'did you go shopping' question and the frustrating setbacks. Each one taught us something valuable not just about tech, but about working with people and building a community."

Their conversation gained momentum as they discussed potential chapters. They envisioned sections on navigating corporate politics, advocating for diversity and inclusion, handling failure with grace, and celebrating successes in ways that motivated entire teams.

Lucy suggested adding a personal touch to each story. "We should also include the less polished moments," she said. "Like how we tackled the initial awkwardness of our mentor-mentee relationship, or how we each dealt with our insecurities about whether we were giving or getting enough value from our sessions."

David nodded, his expression turning thoughtful. "It's important to be authentic. We need to show that building these relationships isn't always smooth sailing, but it's worth the effort. The messy parts are often where the most growth happens. We can cover the clubs we went to, the scenarios we faced, and I'd want to cover how we are not perfect either."

"Exactly that" Lucy responded.

As they planned, they filled a shared digital whiteboard with ideas, themes and sketches of potential chapter titles. They drew out a storyboard, talked to publishers and even imagined a scenario where their book became a Netflix smash hit (please read this Netflix! Or any other streaming company). The excitement was palpable, even through their screens. They discussed including contributions from other industry professionals who could provide additional perspectives on mentorship and support in tech.

"Let's not forget to talk about the practical aspects too," David added. "We can outline strategies for finding the right mentor, initiating meaningful conversations, and setting goals that benefit both the mentor and the mentee."

They discussed the tone of the book, agreeing that it should be a novel but conversational and accessible, much like their own interactions. They wanted to capture the warmth and humour that had characterised their mentorship, ensuring the book felt inviting and encouraging.

As the call neared its end, they reviewed their sprawling web of ideas, feeling both anticipation and determination. They were not just planning a book; they were setting out to influence the culture of an entire industry.

"Lucy, this could be something really special," David said, his voice reflective. "Something that doesn't just recount our personal journey but also inspires a movement within the industry. A movement towards more supportive, understanding and collaborative work environments."

Lucy nodded, her determination clear. "Let's do it, David. Let's write a book that changes the way people think about mentorship and support in the workplace – and beyond. Let's help others build networks that empower and uplift."

With a plan in place and a shared vision that felt ambitious yet utterly necessary, they each felt inspired and ready to tackle the challenge ahead.

Allyship Actually was born.

The days turned into weeks, and weeks into months as Lucy, David and a few carefully selected contributors poured their hearts and souls into crafting the book. Lucy and David spent countless late nights refining each chapter, drawing from their own experiences and those of the professionals who shared their experiences, each of them suffering a form of PTSD as they recounted moments from their lives that should never have happened.

As the publication date loomed closer, anticipation bubbled within them. They knew they were on the cusp of something powerful, something that could spark a revolution in workplace relationships and beyond. The buzz around the book grew, with snippets of their message spreading through the industry like wildfire. Lucy and David were on a journey that even they had not anticipated.

In the future, nobody would ask Lucy if she was here for the shopping.

CHAPTER 38: NEW BEGINNINGS

Lucy

Lucy put her phone down, leant back in her chair and looked out her window. She often did this, when she needed to think or reflect. Although, it really wasn't much of a view outside her window, but at least it was spring and the blossom tree was starting to bloom covering the faded orange brick on the house opposite.

"New beginnings", Lucy thought to herself.

New beginnings, there was something in that. And this was the start of something.

The truth was that Lyra had inspired her to start changing careers. It wasn't the first time Lucy had tried to change her trajectory. When she turned 30, Lucy found her passion for people and psychology – becoming a qualified coach for women in the workplace. Over the years, Lucy has coached hundreds of women, helping many of them to change their careers. Her ambition was to make coaching her full-time career, with speaking opportunities and even securing a few book deals. Prior to this, the time never seemed right to take this leap of faith, and her IT career seemed to hold her back.

It's rather ironic that Lucy had all the tools to change her career, but never utilised them to their full potential.

Lucy couldn't really shy away from the guilt she felt. As much as she had always known that working in IT wasn't her passion, she did try. From trying to turn her coaching practice into a niche for women in tech – something never felt quite right. Furthermore, because she tried so hard, she was in essence, pigeon-holed within this sector.

Or was she?

"It's all too late now!" Lucy cried. "People know me as an ITSM consultant, I have made it into a big deal but I just hate it." Her friend Charlotte, who is a year older than Lucy, but a lot calmer, patiently listened to Lucy as she sobbed again about the career she couldn't escape. Between sobs, Lucy went on saying how she felt like a ginormous failure and that she is going to let people down. Charlotte, as usual, reminded Lucy that she wasn't too old to change her career and she most certainly wasn't a failure.

Lucy admitted to Charlotte that a number of events had led up to this final outburst of desperation. One of them being when Lucy's friend passed away. She was only a few years older than her, married with a newborn baby. Her career path was somewhat similar to Lucy's. She used to work in IT and had held senior roles and because of reasons Lucy will never know, Anne qualified as a coach. That was how Lucy and Anne became friends, when Lucy first explored coaching. Anne was an excellent coach, probably the best coach to have existed. Anne knew things about Lucy that her friends will never know.

In Anne's last message to Lucy, she wrote: "My work as a coach gave my life purpose and in death it will give me peace."

The moment Lucy read that line; tears trickled down her face. Even years after, Lucy thought about Anne often and would repeat her message silently in her head.

Lucy knew she needed to find her purpose and her peace. And she wasn't going to have that being an ITSM consultant.

38: New beginnings

Lucy had joined a six-week programme with the Conde Nast College of Fashion on a fashion branding and communications course. After spending time really considering her own career choices and researching for hours to find her path, it was in front of her the whole time. Lucy had an eye for design. She loves, no, scratch that, adores all elements of branding and design. She also really enjoyed the concept of establishing and growing businesses. That combined, Lucy's ambitions were clear.

She took a trajectory to become a brand and business strategist and her portfolio career allowed her to develop her passion for coaching, writing and speaking.

Maybe, the next time we see Lucy, she could be living in New York City or Milan. She'd take either, really. But for now, she was with David at a conference in London.

CHAPTER 39: ALLYSHIP ACTUALLY

David and Lucy

The conference hall filled with a low hum of expectation as a large and unusually diverse group of professionals looked towards the stage. The vibrant glow of the illuminated screens filled the room as David and Lucy, the keynote speakers at a leadership in business conference, stood waiting to begin their presentation. Their introduction to the stage drew the audience's collective breath of anticipation.

Lucy's beautifully delivered slide deck, 'Allyship Actually,' was a narrative of Lucy and David's working relationship and a powerful tool that symbolised the essence of allyship that they hoped to convey to the audience.

As they had rehearsed over several video calls, David gestured towards his slide, emphatically declaring, "Allyship Actually transcends mere assistance; Lucy has taught me that it's about leveraging our privileges to empower those facing systemic obstacles. Whilst it's true that independent women are undeniably strong, the barriers they confront have deep roots."

A hand shot up from the audience. David and Lucy exchanged the swiftest of knowing glances in preparation for what they thought may come. Uncomfortable questions were par for the course.

"Tell me, why should I intervene? Can't independent women manage themselves?" The man smirked as he waited for an answer, fist-pumping the man to his right.

Lucy and David hid their annoyance. This was because they had grown to expect such a question.

David acknowledged Lucy's nod and took the question, pausing before responding.

"It's true, women possess immense capabilities independently. However, allyship is forging alliances that level the playing field for all. It's about breaking down unjust structures that impede certain groups, it's about using privilege to help those who do not share the same advantage in life; this doesn't just apply to women, it applies to all marginalised groups."

Stepping forward with unwavering confidence, Lucy interjected, "Allyship recognises our interconnected society. When women thrive, entire communities flourish. By being allies, we plant seeds for a fair and prosperous future for all of us." Lucy's resonant voice emphasised the significance of amplifying marginalised voices and fostering inclusivity, reminding the audience of their crucial role in this collective effort.

"No single person can do this alone; it's about we, not me."

David came in as Lucy handed over to him: "Allyship serves as a bridge uniting individuals and opportunities. It propels us towards collective progress by bridging gaps and enabling us to reach new heights together." The audience rippled with applause, slow at first, speeding up as their inquisitor sat back in his chair. This line of questioning further energised the charged atmosphere.

Continuing their session, Lucy and David delved deeper into their actionable steps for incorporating allyship into everyday life, sparking the audience's nods of understanding and note-taking.

39: Allyship Actually

Amidst thunderous applause at the session's conclusion, Lucy and David invited the audience to scan their on-screen QR code to access more learning resources. With that, they began stepping down from the stage. As the applause slowed and people shuffled their papers and prepared to leave, the man who had initially questioned the pair raised his hand again.

David and Lucy were curious to see the raised hand; David asked him, "Do you have a question?"

"No" the man said, taking to his feet. "Please, may I take the microphone?"

David and Lucy were unsure. As insurance, David walked over to the man and handed him the microphone, but held onto it in a vain attempt to control the situation.

The man spoke into the microphone whilst turning to the audience. "Thank you for helping me understand," he said, his voice now sincere and his grin replaced with a look of enlightenment.

"You're welcome." Lucy replied from the stage, smiling.

"One more thing," he said, pausing for effect. "*Allyship Actually,* I get it now. Where do I find out more?"

Lucy and David exchanged knowing glances and nodded in agreement. David gestured to Lucy as he knew that this was her moment.

"Allyship begins with a single step, and we're glad you're taking it with us. Together, we can make a difference."

The man nodded, and as he sat down, he took out his phone and scanned the QR code with a determined look. David and Lucy exchanged a satisfied glance, knowing they had made an impact.

39: Allyship Actually

The applause began again as they wrapped up their session, leaving the stage to a queue of people wanting to learn more.

For David and Lucy, the session proved a success. Getting their message across was important and over the coming months, they saw the attendees act.

The day of the presentation was also the day when *Allyship Actually* was unveiled. After their presentation, David and Lucy found themselves addressing another room filled with eager faces. They spoke not just of their own journey but of the transformative power of allyship and support in every aspect of life. Their words resonated deeply with the audience, igniting a passion for change that seemed to pulse through the air.

As copies of *Allyship Actually* flew off the shelves, testimonials poured in from readers whose lives had been touched by its message. People began forming mentorship connections based on the principles outlined in the book, creating a ripple effect that extended far beyond what David and Lucy had ever imagined.

In the months that followed, *Allyship Actually* became more than just a book; it became a movement. David and Lucy found themselves at the forefront of this shift, working together, speaking at conferences and leading workshops that inspired others to embrace the power of supportive relationships.

As they looked back at their journey, from that first spark of an idea to the widespread impact they had achieved, David and Lucy knew they had accomplished something truly special. They had not only written a book but had sparked a revolution – a revolution built on empathy, understanding, and the unwavering belief that together we can create a world where everyone feels seen, heard and valued.

In the time that passed, Lucy and David found themselves on stage more and more, presenting their stories and those of others, inviting feedback and discovering forms of inequality they hadn't experienced themselves.

Lucy and David knew that their work was far from over. Together, they would continue to champion allyship in all its forms, spreading a message of love and support that would resonate for years to come.

For David, his career as a consultant continued. Now, with the added layer of being seen as an ally who could work in organisations and offer much more than just process or service-based consultancy, he could provide advice on equity and allyship. David continued to work on himself and improve as a human being, knowing full well that his imperfections allowed him to be an authentic ally and understand multiple perspectives.

Lucy was destined for great things. Through co-writing and presenting, Lucy almost unknowingly escaped from the glass box she'd been placed in. No longer constrained by what others chose for her, Lucy thrived as a go-to person, not just for coaching or even her day-to-day role, but as a role model, a disruptor, and a voice for those who had been suppressed and were also looking to break free from their own glass boxes.

For Lucy, this wasn't the end. It was just the beginning.

APPENDIX: THROUGH THEIR VOICES

Saira

From law to tech

I didn't know what allyship was before. Now, having navigated the stormy seas, I wish I had understood its significance earlier in my journey.

As I reflect on my early student days in a corporate law firm, it's impossible to ignore the subtle yet profound challenges that shaped my journey – a journey not just in the legal field (where it all started) but in finding my identity amid a sea of preconceived notions.

From the outset, my experience was tarnished by the mispronunciation of my name. Saira became Sarah at the hands of colleagues who found convenience in the familiarity of the latter. It was more than a mere mispronunciation; it was a dismissal of my identity. Despite correcting them, the phrase "Sarah is easier" persisted, and gradually, I found myself adopting the alias to avoid the constant controversy.

The struggle extended beyond a name; it transcended into a battle for recognition and acceptance. The majority of my colleagues, predominantly white men, unintentionally perpetuated an environment where conformity seemed the only route to professional success.

In this sea of indifference, there was a glimmer of hope – a female lawyer who, in a male-dominated space, I believed would understand the challenges I faced. Unfortunately, reality struck hard during the tumultuous times surrounding the 7/7 London bombings. In a moment when human concern should have prevailed, her response was callous: "Your security isn't my concern, Sarah." It was a painful reminder that empathy and understanding were not guaranteed, even from those who appeared to share a similar struggle.

This incident, coupled with the daily difficulties of assimilation, took a toll on my well-being. The pressure to conform led me to a vasovagal attack (passing out), a physical manifestation of the emotional turmoil within. At 20 years old, I grappled with the paradox of not wanting to die but feeling indifferent to the idea of walking in front of a bus. It was a dark period where my value as an individual seemed diminished in the eyes of those around me.

Years later, having graduated and working as a paralegal, I encountered yet another challenge: a solicitor who harboured resentment from day one. Her dislike towards me was rooted in my recruitment during her maternity leave, and it manifested in constant ridicule of my work, eye rolls and a pointed exclusion from her colloquial endearments, which I was never a recipient of. "Good morning, darling" or "Good morning, hon" were phrases every morning that I would never hear said to me. They were only said to the girls that looked like her.

In sharing my story, I always aim to shed light on the struggles faced by many individuals striving for acceptance and understanding in professional realms. Allyship isn't just about grand gestures; it's about recognising the daily battles faced by those who don't fit the prescribed mould.

My journey underscores the importance of allyship in dismantling the subtle biases that permeate workplaces. It calls for empathy, understanding and a commitment to fostering environments where diverse voices can thrive without compromising their identity.

Amid these challenges, I faced a pivotal crossroads in my career. Despite holding a law degree and completing postgraduate training, the toll of navigating a hostile environment led me to a profound decision – I chose to change careers.

Leaving the legal field was not an abandonment of my passion for justice; instead, it became a conscious choice to prioritise my mental well-being and seek a professional path where my identity and contributions were not constantly under scrutiny. This decision to pivot was not a defeat; rather, it was a reclaiming of my agency and a testament to the resilience forged in the melting pot of adversity.

As I embarked on a new journey in healthcare/tech, I found a space where my voice was heard, my identity celebrated and my skills valued. The transition was a testament to the power of self-advocacy and the importance of recognising when a toxic environment no longer serves one's growth.

My story serves as a reminder that allyship is not solely about weathering storms; it's about fostering environments where individuals can thrive authentically. In sharing my narrative, I hope to inspire others facing similar challenges, urging them to embrace change, prioritise their well-being, and seek environments where their professional journey aligns harmoniously with their personal identity.

My journey from the legal world to a new career path is a testament to the transformative power of self-discovery and resilience. It highlights the crucial need for allyship in the workplace, not just in grand gestures but in the everyday moments that shape our professional and personal lives. We must collectively navigate the complexities of identity and acceptance, and let our individual stories inspire a future where allyship becomes an integral part of the professional landscape, where diversity is not just acknowledged but celebrated.

First and foremost, allyship begins with education. Understanding the nuances of discrimination, sexism and misogyny is crucial for fostering empathy and creating a supportive environment. Take the time to educate yourself on the experiences of those facing adversity and actively listen to their stories.

One practical tip for allies is to amplify marginalised voices. In meetings, discussions or decision-making processes, actively ensure that everyone's perspectives are heard and valued. This not only creates a more inclusive atmosphere but also challenges the status quo, gradually dismantling systemic biases. As an ally, your role is to uplift those whose voices may be drowned out, providing a platform for them to share their insights and experiences.

Addressing microaggressions[42] is another key aspect of effective allyship. These subtle, often unintentional acts of discrimination can accumulate over time, contributing to a toxic environment. Allies can play a crucial role in calling out and addressing these microaggressions when they occur. By doing so, you contribute to a culture where such behaviour is not tolerated, fostering a more inclusive workspace.

---

[42] *https://hbr.org/2022/05/recognizing-and-responding-to-microaggressions-at-work*.

Creating safe spaces for open dialogue is essential. Allyship thrives in an environment where individuals feel comfortable sharing their experiences and concerns. Allyship is about actively engaging in conversations about diversity, equity and inclusion, fostering an atmosphere where colleagues can express themselves without fear of judgement, creating a workplace culture that values authenticity and diverse perspectives.

Acknowledging and rectifying mispronunciations and cultural insensitivity in a tangible way where allies can make a difference. In my own experience, the constant mispronunciation of my name led to a sense of erasure. Allies can actively promote the correct pronunciation of names and challenge any cultural insensitivity within the workplace. This seemingly small gesture contributes significantly to fostering an environment where individuals are respected for their unique identities.

One often overlooked aspect of allyship is advocating for mental health support in the workplace. Allies can use their voices to champion mental health initiatives, ensuring that employees have access to resources and support systems. By acknowledging the impact of workplace dynamics on mental health, allies contribute to a more compassionate and understanding work environment.

Encouraging mentorship and sponsorship programmes within your organisation is another great idea. Allies can play a pivotal role in fostering professional growth for marginalised individuals by actively advocating for mentorship opportunities. Mentorship provides guidance, support and a network that can be invaluable for navigating the complexities of a challenging workplace. Allies can actively promote and participate in such programmes, contributing to a more equitable professional landscape. I am proud to have mentored women who are now making change in their own communities and organisations, and what has really helped has been sharing stories such as these.

Lastly, allyship is an ongoing journey, not a one-time effort. We should all stay informed about evolving issues related to diversity and inclusion. Actively seek feedback from those you aim to support, and be open to learning from your mistakes. Allyship requires a commitment to continual improvement and adaptation. By staying engaged and responsive, allies can contribute to a workplace culture that values diversity, champions inclusivity, and actively works towards dismantling systemic biases.

Allyship, as I have now come to understand it, is a deeply personal and transformative journey for each and every one of us. From education to amplification, from addressing microaggressions to fostering open dialogue, each aspect of allyship is a thread in the tapestry of creating a workplace where every single person feels valued and respected. These practical tips from my very own experiences throughout the years will hopefully serve as a guide for allies to contribute to a more inclusive and equitable professional landscape that recognises the power of individual stories and the strength that comes from unity.

Samantha

*B*tch, the real story*

"Everyone thinks you must be a b*tch to have gotten that job, but I actually think you're quite nice."

We were at the work Christmas party shortly after my promotion had been announced. I was in my early 20s and had got a place on a news desk.

It was, admittedly, unusual for a woman of my age (or any age) to be on a news desk.

My boss told me how his decision to promote me was met with some derision and confusion.

Like anyone rising to the challenge of a promotion, I was filled with nerves.

But the woman next to me at the party who said this (after a couple of festive tipples), was in another department, and had never spoken to me before.

There were two things that struck me.

First, the assumption that a woman getting ahead at work must be through what we think of as 'b*tchy' behaviour.

Second, the importance of being seen as 'nice'. There is an emphasis on nicety for women in leadership that is absent from the qualities we look for in male leaders.

Male leaders are seen as bold and strong if they display a set of qualities that are considered stern and cold in women.

For some context: I had been in newsrooms since I was 16 years old.

That's because I grew up in Paulsgrove, a council estate in Portsmouth, and I didn't know anyone in the media.

No one in my family had been to university. My dad worked four jobs simultaneously at one point to put food on the table, so being a journalist felt like somewhat of an impossibility for me.

But I loved to tell stories, I loved to write, and most importantly I had what I now know is a strong conviction to help people.

When you grow up in an environment like that, you see things. The impact of long-term, generational poverty, lack of investment, the use of alcohol and drugs to numb pain.

One of my earliest memories is a fight outside the shopping precinct in broad daylight, one man smashing another's head against the pavement.

Aside from an elderly lady who swung her handbag at them (which I'm pretty certain was full of bricks), my mum was the only person to get involved and pull them apart.

It sounds like a cliché, but I wanted to become a journalist to *do* something. I witnessed how kids I grew up with, many of whom had much more of an aptitude than me for things like maths and science, were increasingly despondent.

They started skipping school and smoking weed when they were 11. And is it any wonder when no one showed any belief in them?

The teachers did not believe in us either. Despite the knife fights that were happening right there in the corridors, the teachers would often turn up to class late, one of them then proceeding to sit reading the paper.

My parents got called in to see the head because my English teacher thought I must have plagiarised the poem I handed in for homework; she did not believe a kid from here could write like that and she told my parents as much.

My mum lied about our address to get me into a better school several miles away as she could see I was becoming jaded.

We couldn't afford all the fancy uniform for my new school in a nicer borough.

I was bullied relentlessly for being from Paulsgrove.

One day during PE, someone stole all my uniform from the changing rooms.

For any parent, that's annoying.

For mine, it meant making choices about what we could eat so they had the money to replace it.

If you didn't wear the required items, you were suspended.

While the teachers were present and the education was delivered, I was nicknamed 'Council Estate Sam.'

One girl, who lived in a mansion and would invite me round likely so her family could gawp and feel like they were doing something charitable, used to tell me "you're never going to move off the council estate."

Journalism is a notoriously elitist industry – *"According to the Sutton Trust, 80% of editors went to private school; only 11% of journalists are from working-class backgrounds, and a measly 0.2% of journalists are Black."*[43] In 2022, a further study found working-class representation in the media hit a record low, and 42 per cent of journalists were from higher class backgrounds.[44] Measures to try and redress the balance include apprenticeships. These eliminate the need for a degree to get into a paid position. But given that salaries for

---

[43] *https://www.theguardian.com/media/2024/apr/04/new-journalism-school-in-london-sets-out-to-improve-black-representation*.

[44] *https://pressgazette.co.uk/media-audience-and-business-data/journalists-class-backgrounds/*.

journalism apprentices hits around £11,000, or less in some cases, its near impossible without family support.

As I write, the average cost of living in the UK is more than £25,000.[45]

To get through university, I worked two jobs. I then had to get a qualification called the NCTJ Diploma. Many publishers make this mandatory because there are lots of laws governing UK media, and the qualification gives some assurance that you won't get your editor sued or jailed.

At the time, it cost around £2000 to study for this qualification at an accredited centre (Highbury College).

In 2024, the fees are still prohibitively high for many. To take the four 'essential' exams to qualify for the Certificate for Foundation Journalism (distance learning), you can expect to pay £465 plus VAT.

This does not include the court reporting qualification.

The NCTJ says the average cost per student for the Diploma [different to the certificate] distance learning is £365.

This includes only one hour of tutor support.[46]

If publishers won't take you without these qualifications and you do not have family support, these fees present a significant hurdle.

Then there is the industry insistence that you must have work experience to be considered for a paid role.

---

[45] *https://abcfinance.co.uk/blog/the-true-cost-of-living-in-uk-cities/*.

[46] *https://www.nctj.com/qualifications-courses/qualifications/*.

For someone whose parents can support them during work experience, fine. For someone who needs to get paid to live, this creates a barrier.

I cleaned toilets, worked as a housemaid, was a lettings agent on weekends and even worked in a pharmaceutical factory to fund my way through this diploma and unpaid internships.

When I finally got an interview for a paid role (I had to take two trains to get there, which is a big deal when every penny counts), I spent my last £30 on an outfit.

I was wearing a raspberry-coloured shift dress and a black blazer.

And I was told by the editor: "I think you're too into fashion to be a serious news journalist."

I had to write FIVE full-page stories that were worthy of the front-end of the paper to prove myself, despite the many cuttings I'd brought with me.

None of my male counterparts were asked to do this.

Making ends meet on a low salary as well as being required to run a car for the job is tough.

I often had very little money left to buy groceries and other necessities for the week.

Fast-forward to the Christmas party, when I had worked so unbelievably hard to get on news desk, only to have someone I had never spoken to telling me I was seen as a b*tch.

The irony!

You're either too into fashion, or you're a b*tch.

You either make no effort and are seen as unserious, or care about what you wear and are seen as vacuous.

People judge you based on your gender and the way you dress and not on your merit.

And they don't consider the struggle it took for you to get into the room in the first place.

During my time in newsrooms, I had come to see certain traits as 'the norm'; often editors (usually male) were stressed and shouting.

They were 'do-not-approach-before-coffee' figures who had to be given bad news gently, lest they tear down the entire office.

I had witnessed one kick a bin across a newsroom, another scream at employees; I'd actually been slapped myself a couple of times across the back of the head.

But whenever the behaviour of this type of man came up in hushed conversations, it was always with the caveat "he's so stressed/he has such a tough job."

Before I had officially begun my stint on the news desk, people were already assuming I must be a 'b*tch' for even getting there.

It was clear to me that even though I aimed to do things differently than how I'd seen them done before, I would not be given the grace extended to others.

What I didn't know at the time of that Christmas party conversation was how often in the future, as my career progressed, I'd be the subject of these kinds of remarks. Or how many times I'd walk into the room and be mistaken for a note-taker.

When I was collecting an award a few years ago, the presenter wouldn't hand it over; he looked at me with bemusement – it took my male deputy coming to the stage and confirming that yes, this little lady was in charge, for him to let me have it.

Educating white cis men who have for centuries been used to being the dominant voice in the room is one thing.

The job in that case is to open up their perspective so they realise all of this, and give them the opportunity to change.

And many (in my experience) are keen to learn.

But when misogyny comes another woman? That's a different challenge.

One of the worst events I've ever been to was exclusively for women in journalism. I was there with a small group of peers around my age, and we were made to feel like aliens.

The tension in the air was palpable and more than one barbed comment was made about someone's appearance.

I think that's because when there is only one seat at the table for women, patriarchal conditioning makes us want to fight for it. Instead, we should build more chairs, or a bigger, better table.

Recently, I was speaking to a recruiter who told me a candidate was turned down because they were wearing 'the wrong colour shoes'.

As the recruiter pointed out, the candidate was from a background like mine and could barely afford the shoes.

I would love interviewing managers to be more considerate of people's differences, and to also provide robust guidance on dress codes.

And to go back as far as the school system, I would love policymakers to think more carefully about mandatory uniform rules that discriminate against those who can't afford them, and those who are neurodivergent and may have issues with certain materials or labels.

When a client of mine got a new job not long ago, they saw that the welcome pack said "Use your common sense."

This is grossly inadequate.

'Common sense' is subjective and does not take into consideration different people's experiences, beliefs or needs.

It's a phrase that instantly excludes because different cultures have different common practices and customs.

Not to mention that state schools do not prepare students properly for work.

Nor is everyone exposed to corporate culture via their parents or the environment in which they grow up.

But there is also research that shows that women are still judged on what they're wearing in a way that men are not.

In 2014, a male Australian news anchor wore the same suit on air for a year and no one noticed.[47]

In 2024, anchors at a Canadian station decided to see if things had changed a decade on. The male newsreaders garnered no comments but the female newsreaders did.[48]

---

[47] *https://www.cbsnews.com/news/karl-stefanovic-australian-tv-anchor-wore-same-suit-for-one-year-and-no-one-noticed/*.

[48] *https://globalnews.ca/news/10263239/global-news-anchors-wardrobe-experiment/*.

Allyship doesn't only look like men supporting women in the workplace; it also looks like women supporting women, and us all supporting those who identify in other ways.

It means thinking about the socio-economic differences.

It means that when we get in the room, we must look around and ask, "Who ISN'T here?"

It means considering the needs of others over our own.

It means handing over the microphone and actually listening to the lived experiences of others, not pretending to listen for a PR exercise.

It looks like challenging assumptions and stepping into conversations to correct stereotypes.

It means asking, when being invited to speak at events or to contribute to projects like this, "Who else is involved?"

And most importantly, it means challenging our own assumptions and beliefs.

Farah

Sexual harassment

My career has been anything but conventional. Spanning continents from Africa to the Middle East and Europe, I've navigated the complexities of many industries where being a woman, let alone an Asian woman in leadership, is a rarity. Starting young and climbing the ranks swiftly, I founded my own company, challenging the status quo at every turn.

Yet, life isn't without its curveballs. There was a period when I found myself at a crossroads, dialling back from leadership roles to navigate personal health challenges. This detour was illuminating – not just about my resilience but also the shifts in perception and treatment I experienced stepping away from the helm.

Sexual harassment, unfortunately, has been a constant shadow in my professional journey, irrespective of my role or the country I was in. Initially, like many, I lacked the tools and the voice to effectively counter it. But with time, my toolkit expanded and my resolve strengthened. Through projects like Catcalls of London and my contributions to multiple violence against women and girls' initiatives and forums, I've turned my experiences into platforms for advocacy and education on consent, community and combatting sexual harassment. It's about fostering a culture of allyship and understanding, challenging the norms, and maybe, just maybe, making the path a little easier for the next person who walks it.

The chapter of my career that I refer to as the 'crossroads' wasn't marked by a signpost; it was more of an abrupt halt, a forced pause instigated by a brush with a cancer scare and the daunting realisation that I was grappling with complex PTSD. These weren't just hurdles; they were colossal mountains that suddenly appeared on a path I had been confidently navigating.

Deciding to step back wasn't easy. It felt counterintuitive, like I was retreating from a battlefield I had dominated. I transitioned to roles that, on paper, seemed a few rungs lower on the ladder. But this wasn't about defeat; it was about strategy, about giving myself the space to heal and regroup – though at the time it felt like anything but.

The professional landscape from this new vantage point was starkly different. The authoritative voice that once commanded teams and drove initiatives was now part of the chorus, often struggling to be heard. The respect and autonomy I was accustomed to in leadership positions seemed conditional, tied more to the title than the expertise. It was a sobering reminder of the fragile nature of professional stature and the shifting dynamics of workplace respect.

Navigating this phase, I was acutely aware of the change in treatment and attitudes. It was like watching a play from a different seat in the theatre – the lines were the same, but the angles and the lighting revealed different facets, some less flattering than others. This wasn't just about personal battles with health; it was a litmus test for my professional environment, highlighting disparities and biases that were less visible from the top.

From the remote sites of Congo, where the threat was so palpable that a knife under my pillow felt like a necessary precaution, to the polished offices of government ministers, the spectre of harassment was ever-present. It morphed from overt dangers to subtler, insidious pressures – from colleagues coaxing me to have "just one more" drink, to the all-too-familiar dance around inappropriate comments and the dodging of wandering hands.

Appendix: Through their voices

In my early years, I was armed with little more than a determined spirit to face these challenges. The tools and knowledge to effectively counter such behaviours were not part of my arsenal, nor were they readily available. The landscape of awareness and resources for dealing with sexual harassment was markedly different, leaving me to rely on instinct and, at times, sheer force of will to maintain my boundaries and professionalism.

Over time, my understanding of and response to these incidents have undergone a significant transformation. With each encounter, I gleaned insights not just about the perpetrators and the environments that embolden them but also about myself – my strengths, my vulnerabilities and my resolve to advocate for change. The experiences, as harrowing as they were, became catalysts for growth and action.

I learned to harness my voice, not just for my own defence but as a beacon for others who might find themselves in similar situations. From a defensive posture, I moved to an offensive one, aiming to alter the dynamics that perpetuate such behaviours.

Projects like Catcalls of London and the development of security industry-specific recommendations on addressing sexual harassment are testaments to this evolution. What started in 2017 as a campaign to highlight public sexual harassment has burgeoned into a multifaceted advocacy platform spearheading numerous international initiatives. However, the heart of this work has been the workshops conducted with young people across the UK, aimed at fostering a deeper understanding of consent, community and the nuances of harassment.

Parallel to this, my immersion in the security industry unveiled a disconcerting reality – that the pervasiveness of sexual harassment was not just anecdotal but systemic. This realisation spurred the development of a comprehensive study, culminating in a set of recommendations tailored for the industry. The objective was clear: to illuminate the shadows where such behaviours thrive and to chart a course towards a more respectful and safe professional environment.

The cornerstone of my advocacy lies in the conviction that knowledge is not just power, it's protection. Educating individuals of all ages to identify sexual harassment is the first step in dismantling the mechanisms that perpetuate it. But awareness alone isn't enough. Equipping people with the tools to advocate for themselves and others transforms passive knowledge into active defence and support.

This dual approach of education and empowerment is pivotal. It's not merely about addressing incidents post-factum but about cultivating an environment where respect and dignity are non-negotiable, where harassment is not just recognised but is actively resisted and condemned. Through workshops, campaigns and policy recommendations, the goal is to embed these principles into our communities and workplaces, fostering a culture where allyship is not just a concept but a lived practice.

Throughout my career, particularly during its most testing periods, the concept of allyship often felt more like an ideal than a tangible reality. In the high-stakes environments and the diverse cultural contexts where I worked, admitting vulnerability seemed tantamount to professional hara-kiri. The solitude in these moments wasn't chosen; it was a byproduct of the unwritten codes of conduct that equated strength with stoicism and independence with invincibility.

This isolation, while profoundly challenging, underscored a critical gap in the ecosystems I navigated – a lack of structured support and empathy for those in distress. It wasn't that compassion or solidarity didn't exist, but the mechanisms to express and enact them were underdeveloped, often stifled by the fear of appearing weak or undermining one's authority.

My experiences, while personally disheartening, ignited a resolve to ensure others wouldn't have to endure similar solitude. Advocacy for others, therefore, became not just a component of my work; it evolved into its cornerstone. I recognised that creating a more inclusive and respectful professional environment required more than just addressing overt acts of discrimination or harassment. It necessitated cultivating a culture where seeking help was seen as a sign of prudence, not weakness, and where offering support was a default response, not a heroic act.

The importance of support, empathy and understanding in any professional setting cannot be overstated. These are not just soft skills or nice-to-have attributes but are foundational to building resilient, dynamic and cohesive teams. An environment that champions these values is one where individuals can thrive, not despite their vulnerabilities, but alongside them. It's about shifting the paradigm from surviving to thriving, from solitary struggles to collective triumphs.

In advocating for a culture steeped in allyship, I aim to dismantle the barriers that keep us isolated in our challenges. By fostering a professional ethos that prizes empathy and support as much as competence and achievement, we pave the way for a more inclusive, respectful and ultimately more effective workplace.

The tapestry of my professional journey, embroidered with challenges, triumphs and myriad lessons, underscores a fundamental truth: the path to change is both personal and collective. Each encounter with discrimination, each battle with personal demons, and every step taken towards advocacy and education has been a brick in the foundation of a larger edifice – one built on the principles of respect, empathy and allyship.

From the stark realities of workplace harassment to the solitude of personal battles, the journey has been as instructive as it has been challenging. The key lessons are clear: resilience is invaluable, vulnerability is not a weakness, and the pursuit of change, while often solitary, has the power to resonate and inspire collective action.

To those navigating similar paths, my advice is straightforward: embrace your journey with both its trials and triumphs. Let your experiences, however daunting, be your guide and not your shackles. Remember, the strength to advocate for change, to champion allyship, begins with the courage to confront the uncomfortable, to challenge the status quo, and to extend a hand, whether in search of support or to offer it.

Becoming better allies in our personal and professional lives is not just about grand gestures; it's found in the everyday acts of kindness, in the willingness to listen and in the courage to speak up. It's about building bridges where walls once stood, about turning empathy into action, and about recognising that our individual strengths are amplified when we stand together.

I encourage you, the reader, to embrace allyship as a fundamental part of who you are and how you interact with the world. It's not about grandiose gestures but the consistent, everyday choices that contribute to a culture of respect, empathy and support. Let's work together to make these values not just aspirational but the standard in both our personal and professional spheres.

Ima

LGBTQI+

I have been a transsexual all my life. Nothing to be 'proud' about, it's just how it is. From my early childhood, my parents were puzzled, thinking that my being a girl was a phase that would pass, though strangers less so, but my girlish appearance let me get away with pretending to be a girl without too much trying.

Don't get me wrong, it was never about 'wanting to be a girl', and I wasn't always particularly happy about being perceived as one. It just so happened that girls bonded with me more often and I kept on ending up in their camp, especially when we had to face our common adversaries – boys – in games and fights and, later, relationships. It went so far that the 'Best Man' at my wedding was a girl and I later on was invited to two weddings as a 'Maid of Honour'.

Nevertheless, I tried to please my parents and be more boyish in my games and behaviour – which would often result in being told off by some elderly person on the bus for "not behaving as good girls should." So, yes, a fairly confusing childhood and plenty of 'junior-aimed misogyny', along with being regularly stalked and once actually sexually attacked on public transport, all of which have inevitably shaped my vision of myself and the world around me.

We were taught in those days not to see ourselves as victims and even to be ashamed if we allowed someone to victimise us, so we were cheerfully stepping over such experiences and carrying on, trying to make a success of ourselves. It wasn't that easy; unless you had complied with the societal norms and fitted all the boxes of your expected behaviour, you had a very little chance to progress. And those accepting their condition, with or without doctors' involvement, had quite a limited choice of careers – a model, an actress, an escort, a dominatrix, a bearded lady (just kidding, this last one wasn't a thing in those days!). Nevertheless, these were mostly risky, seedy professions. I knew transsexual girls with two or three diplomas in serious professional subjects from prestigious universities, speaking half a dozen foreign languages, and yet all they could do was work as an escort or an exotic dancer.

So, we were sort of relieved when at last, following many years of social activism, our basic human rights were acknowledged and we were allowed to work alongside our more complacent colleagues. But then the corporations started to compete with each other in accommodating LGBTQ+ people, which led inevitably to the most ridiculous cases of 'rainbow-washing' (a term coined in the 1980s, but more in use since 2010s).

Rainbow-washing is all about claiming to be an LGBTQ+ ally while using it to appear morally superior to competitors, and yet often sending confusing, controversial or conflicting messages and/or supporting openly anti-LGBTQ+ entities and initiatives. Nearly every major multinational corporation at least once got into a situation like that. Despite their wealth of resources and easily available legal advice, brands like M&S, Starbucks, FedEx, Amazon, Ford, Toyota, Nike and Google were all accused of rainbow-washing.

Want to see first-hand some real-life examples? Just take a stroll in June, aka Pride Month, in central London or any other megapolis, and you'll immediately spot big-shot companies going all out with rainbow flags and LGBTQ+ shoutouts in their logos and ads. But let's be real: the rest of the year, many of them are often 'missing the action' in supporting LGBTQ+ causes, including their own crew. These same guys roll out LGBTQ+ campaigns and materials without even asking their LGBTQ+ team or having any LGBTQ+ representation up on their executive board.

I was hired like that – by large global corporations – only to figure out they wanted me for the LGBTQ+ badge rather than my actual skills and experience, which sort of defies the whole idea, devalues our experiences and newly gained social rights. I won't wear your badges with pronouns, I want to be respected as a professional.

If you're talking about being a true friend to the LGBTQ+ crew, it's all about keeping it real across the board, not just slapping rainbows on things for show. And let's go beyond the surface-level stuff. Companies should actually step up and make life better for LGBTQ+ folks – that means real policies and support, not just some glossy image. And inside the company, different teams should work together making sure everyone knows the deal when it comes to supporting LGBTQ+.

To be real LGBTQ+ allies, corporations also need to toughen up against any public backlash. Don't fold under pressure – stick to your guns and show unwavering commitment to LGBTQ+ rights. It's about weathering storms like boycotts and hate campaigns without budging.

It's also about creating a workplace that's discrimination-free. Companies should go beyond lip service and put their money where their mouth is. Implement and enforce a zero-tolerance policy against any kind of bullying. This isn't just about having a policy on paper; it's about making sure every employee feels safe and respected, with no exceptions. A workplace free from discrimination is the foundation for a genuinely supportive environment.

Dealing with employees who might not be on board with LGBTQ+ acceptance can be tough. Some may just feel uncomfortable with working with openly LGBTQ+ colleagues, others may be self-confessed bigots. But instead of just ordering them to behave and pushing them to conform, how about a little education? Corporations should take the lead by offering in-depth training programmes and casual get-togethers with LGBTQ+ folks. These gatherings aren't about ticking boxes; they're about boosting awareness and understanding of LGBTQ+ issues, making the workplace way more inclusive.

We mustn't forget the basics, however – being straight up, transparent, is key. Companies set to forge genuine allyship should engage with their LGBTQ+ staff regularly, get their take on company rules, and make sure decisions have everyone's best interests at heart.

Depending on how far and deep you want to go in your allyship, you may also consider shaking things up in the corporate decision-making game. The LGBTQ+ community always needs a real seat at the big table – no less than any other underrepresented group – so are you ready to put LGBTQ+ folks on the executive board? Let their voices shape company policies because, let's face it, authentic perspectives come from those who've walked the walk.

Another important aspect – promote integration, not demands for special treatment, for it is the secret sauce for a workplace where everyone feels at home. Corporations should talk more about our shared human values among all employees, pushing for a culture that's all about acceptance and inclusion. Let's keep it chill and focus on everyone feeling like they belong. Embrace the humanity we all share. Make it a place where everyone's cool with who they are.

And while corporations should be all about equity, they must also keep it real and never lose their guard. Find that sweet spot between fairness and common sense to avoid any exploitation. Striking a balance ensures the company stays sharp against folks who might fake an LGBTQ+ identity for personal gain or ulterior motives.

Token gestures and stereotyping? Let's leave all that behind. Companies should hire staff based on skills, not just to fill a diversity checklist. LGBTQ+ folks aren't props – we've got our own personalities and bring something unique to the table.

Consulting with big LGBTQ+ advocacy groups is cool, but why not cast a wider net? Talk to a bunch of different LGBTQ+ organisations, embracing the diversity within the community. It's not a one-size-fits-all deal, and recognising that ensures a more genuine and inclusive approach to allyship.

Navigating the LGBTQ+ allyship journey might be tricky, but we can skip the fancy stuff, the make-believe, and just be real and kind. It's not about show, it's about making the workplace genuinely awesome for everyone and accepting everyone for who they are. And not demanding from them to state who or what they identify as or not identify at all. Drop the badges with pronouns – unless they make someone happy – then, by all means, let them wear them, with pride or without.

Let's not forget to be humans – warm and kind, remembering how much we share, how closely we all are related and ignoring any awkward or unpleasant things that separate or divide us. Be kind – it's all that matters.

ABOUT THE AUTHORS – WHO WE REALLY ARE

Hi, I'm Lucy.

It is rather ironic that alongside all the things I have done and continue to do, I am co-writing a book. You see, I couldn't read until I was 11. This was a combination of a tricky childhood mixed with an assumption that I had learning difficulties. If you ask my stepfather, he will tell you that I was lazy. If you ask me, I will tell you that is half true, but equally the system was against me. Which is somewhat of a theme in my life and career.

I will always remember that teacher who told my mum that I would never be able to read words that have more than four letters in them. And then there was this other teacher who predicted that I would get all Es in my GCSEs – I got two Bs in his subject. And then there was that moment when my childhood boyfriend told me that I didn't have any ambition.

Coming from a working-class family, I watched my mum figure out ways to get food on the table.

However, as a single mum on benefits, this made us vulnerable. Then add in the high-school bullying – is it any wonder that I couldn't read?

I have carried depression as part of me since the age of five. This isn't an exaggeration; it's a fact. I have thought about and tried (more than once) to take my life and been in and out of therapy since 2007.

It's been since 2020, during the pandemic, believe it or not, where I have finally healed. I finally feel like I have something to live for.

Why do I share this with you?

As a white, middle-class woman, I understand my privilege. But, as you've just read, I wasn't given these opportunities, I had to work hard and create them. So I want to do something with this privilege. To make change. To be change.

Being a woman, my career has been – how can I put this – interesting. I have had some shocking managers. I have had some terrible jobs. And I have had my fair share of sexist jokes that were disguised as banter.

Yet, on a positive note, how lucky am I to have worked in leading industries and creative brands? I've been able to travel and be on secret projects – but at what cost?

The stories in this book are all from real moments in all of our careers. You might think some sections have been 'Hollywoodified' for a dramatic effect. They haven't. The only things we have done is changed names, timeframes and tailored scenarios to protect both ourselves and other people.

So, go write a book, they said.

It is a relief to work with a male where there isn't an ulterior motive (and if I could, I'd include a side eye emoji here). David isn't the first man I have worked with who has offered friendship and support. Ian, Dave, Julian and Scott all have too. Then there is Jim, another Dave and Alan...

I have to take a moment here to say thank you to my mum and my stepdad. My mum taught me a lot of life lessons and didn't take no for an answer when it came to me and my education. My stepdad identified there was a 'problem' and on his lunch break, he would go to WH Smith and bring me back those books I hated that taught me maths, English and science. I hated them so much, but without them, I wouldn't have realised my potential. Thank you for believing in me.

Hi, I'm David, aka Dar.

I come from a 'broken' childhood, but not in the way you'd expect. I was never harmed, mistreated, or abused – far from it.

But I also didn't feel loved, cherished, or even encouraged. During my first ten years on this earth, my family moved many times, due to my father's work. My father was often overseas, working for months, and my mother did her best at home and in unfamiliar surroundings.

Still, years later, when she died from illnesses relating to alcoholism, it became obvious to me that she'd struggled with her demons from way before I was born. As a child, I often felt alone. As an adult, I blame my mother's alcoholism for this, which burns me inside.

I'd be cheery on the outside, always meeting up with people and playing sports, but I would look at the sidelines and see nobody there to support me. Today, that motivates me to succeed, but it makes me uncomfortable about accepting praise.

My overriding memory of my sporting activities wasn't winning sports day sprints or scoring goals (mainly because I rarely did); it was one day seeing my father on the sideline and scoring an own goal. It killed me.

When I was ten, my parents decided to set up a base in a small town in the north of England. This was because I'd been to several primary schools by then, including one in Northern Ireland where kids and teachers bullied me. My response to that had been to wrap myself up in my own thoughts. None of the bullying had been vicious – I wasn't beaten too badly, but I didn't fight back either. I just soaked it in.

Secondary school was great; my mates from there are still my friends to this day. We were and still are of similar spirit. We played together, shared the same interests and none of us really tried that hard. We didn't need to; school was just a chance to smoke, play football and have fun. All of us have gone on to be successful in our own way.

Those friends gave me a band of brothers and sisters I'd never had before. I had female friends who were just that. We'd hang out, support one another and pass comments on how good we looked.

It was fun, and I'm proud to have those female friends to this very day. Seeing them as successful adults at work and/or as mothers and partners is great.

Leaving school was brilliant. We came from a small town, and I was already familiar with most of the pubs, and at 16, that extended to the rave scene. I mention this because I really believe it formed me into who I am today. Getting involved in that scene – and its drugs – opened my mind to a world of possibilities. I met 'types' of people I would never have ordinarily met by travelling around the country in various states (both of clothing and inebriation). We had a wild time, but I learned a lot about character, trust, faith, empathy, love and the media, who portrayed the scene as people eating bat heads and zombies. Mate, you don't eat much when you are off your nut, and certainly not bats.

All this happened as I forged a promising career in tech, but you can read about that on LinkedIn.

Ultimately, who I am is that kid at home on his own, dreaming of being praised. I'm that boy on the sports field wishing the ground would swallow him up; I'm that wide-eyed youth on the dance floor of Cream in Liverpool, hugging and being hugged among hundreds of strangers, discovering that the world is multicoloured, multi-faceted, and not the black-and-white options I was presented with until that point.

I'm also a male that isn't naturally confident nor naturally gifted – but I'll work damn hard to get where I want to be, or to help others get to where they want or need to be. This is down to two things I need to thank my mother and father for. First, my mother's addictive personality has manifested itself in many ways in my life. I now harness it; if I'm in, you better believe I'm all in, feet first, followed by all of me. Second, my father is the hardest worker in the room. For this, I thank you both.

Our views on Allyship

If you look up the term 'ally', you'll find multiple definitions.

The one that resonates the most with us is the Merriam-Webster definition:

> *"One that is associated with another as a helper; a person or group that provides assistance and support in an ongoing effort, activity or struggle."*

Allyship isn't a trend, or a label, or even something new.

It also isn't just about hiring more 'diverse' people (to tick your corporate box).

It is an important position whereby the ally is making sure that everyone, especially marginalised people, are not only invited to have a seat at the table but they also have a voice and a contribution.

It is about challenging the status quo.

And being part of the solution (taking action) and not the problem.

It seems like a lot, but really it isn't. Yet, it would be wrong to say it was simple.

There will always be blockers from both internal and external factors. There'll be people that have opinions that don't match your values and you'll have questions around the approach.

In terms of men being allies and sponsors for women, the below sums it up nicely:

"Would-be male allies may struggle to identify subtle forms of sexism or exclusion at work and fear backlash when they speak out. Research suggests that men may be unsure how to be an ally and have trouble navigating power dynamics at work. But a commitment to equity, as well as support from other men, can help motivate men to act as allies…

…When men speak up on behalf of women, they're more likely to be taken seriously by other men. As a result, women who have experienced sexism or oppression feel more confident and empowered. According to a new study, women who believe they have strong allies at work feel a

greater sense of inclusion and more energy and enthusiasm on the job."[49]

When researching and writing this book, we found common themes that were stopping men from becoming allies:

- Men feel that they don't want to overstep their boundaries.
- Men worry about what other people will say.
- Lad-led cultures prevent men from stepping up.
- Imposter syndrome.

Why are male allies important for women in the workplace? They can support progress towards gender equity across all levels.

They can proactively question and challenge behaviours. Starting in their own circles then reaching out further.

They should then look to carry some of the accountability for creating change within industries and workplaces. It isn't about being a male saviour and isn't all on them, just like it isn't all on us.

It is a collaborative effort.

It's about bringing in balance to drive inclusive cultures forward.

By actively getting involved in supporting and encouraging female colleagues in multiple guises from mentoring to

---

[49] *https://www.mindful.org/why-male-allyship-matters-in-the-workplace/*.

leading to teaching and so forth, women are starting to share a piece of that pie that is often so hard for them to reach.

This is being inclusive.

And guess what?

There is a return of investment here.

Building diversity in the workplace means better business. FACT.

And from a personal development point of view, the male ally will experience a level of growth, gain knowledge and will be on their own learning journeys.

So, where to start?

Over the last few years, there have been some exciting developments in the DE&I space. But there is a lot of information out there. Thus, it is often hard to know where to begin. In the Resources section, there are some of our suggestions.

RESOURCES

If you would like to reach out to us to discuss the book/anything allyship related, please send us an email:

- *lucyanddavid@allyshipactually.com*

For more information about us, visit our Linktree page:

- *https://linktr.ee/allyshipresources*

If you have been impacted by what has been written in this book, please do consult your doctor for recommendations via your local mental health support. Additional mental health support can be found via:

- BetterHelp: *https://Betterhelp.com*
- Andy's Man Club: *https://andysmanclub.co.uk/*

If you also need help with a scenario mentioned in this book, the following organisations will provide you with support:

- Reporting rape in the UK: *https://www.gov.uk/report-rape-sexual-assault*

- Reporting harassment in the UK: Contact your local police force

- Questions or concerns on workplace rights, rules and best practice: *https://www.acas.org.uk/*

- UN Women: *https://www.unwomen.org/en*

- Equality Act: *https://www.gov.uk/guidance/equality-act-2010-guidance*

- Mind Out – LGBTQ Mental Health Service: *https://mindout.org.uk/*

Insightful communities:

- Women of ITSM Community: *https://www.linkedin.com/groups/2133634/*
- Reed Women in Technology Mentoring Programme: *https://resources.reed.com/women-in-technology-mentoring-programme*
- Men Partnering for Change: *https://www.linkedin.com/groups/14520729/*

Books:

- *Why Men Win at Work* by Gill Whitty-Collins
- *Invisible Women: Exposing Data Bias in a World Designed for Men* by Caroline Criado Perez
- *Lean In: Women, Work, and the Will to Lead* by Sheryl Sandberg
- *F*ck Being Humble* by Stefanie Sword-Williams
- *Financial Feminist* by Tori Dunlap
- *The Guilty Feminist* by Deborah Frances-White
- *Fix the System, Not the Women* by Laura Bates
- *Women Don't Owe You Pretty* by Florence Given
- *Feminist Don't Wear Pink (and other lies)* by Scarlett Curtis
- *The Second Sex* by Simone de Beauvoir

Podcasts:

Resources

- *WSJ Secrets of Wealthy Women?*: https://www.wsj.com/podcasts/secrets-of-wealthy-women
- *The Guilty Feminist*: https://guiltyfeminist.com/
- *Talk Female Friday Podcast: Allyship with Dave*: https://podcasters.spotify.com/pod/show/talkfemalefridaypodcast/episodes/Episode-69-Allyship-with-Dave-Rice-e1shvp2
- *IT's all about Choices – An Allyship Special*: https://www.youtube.com/watch?v=wjo1mrc2LWQ&t=15s

Documentaries/films:

- *Miss Representation* (documentary): https://www.imdb.com/title/tt1784538/
- *Bombshell* (film): https://www.imdb.com/title/tt6394270/
- *She Said* (film): https://www.imdb.com/title/tt11198810/

LinkedIn learning:

- Becoming an ally to all: https://www.linkedin.com/learning/becoming-an-ally-to-all?
- Leading your org on a journey of allyship: https://www.linkedin.com/learning/leading-your-org-on-a-journey-of-allyship

- Supporting allyship and anti-racism at work: *https://www.linkedin.com/learning/supporting-allyship-and-anti-racism-at-work?*

Articles:

- Power skills: *https://toggl.com/blog/power-skills*
- Microaggressions: *https://www.imperial.ac.uk/media/imperial-college/faculty-of-engineering/public/Resource---Examples-of-Microaggressions.pdf*
- Be a better ally *https://hbr.org/2020/11/be-a-better-ally*
- 7 Ways to practice active allyship *https://hbr.org/2022/11/7-ways-to-practice-active-allyship*

Allyship Actually coaching exercise for people leaders and teams

These coaching questions are designed to spark reflection, exploration, and growth between leaders and their people/teams. We recommend that you:

1. Book a meeting with your team member for 30-60 minutes. Create a psychological safe space by explaining that this is a session for you both to listen and learn.
2. At the start of your session explain to your team member about the coaching exercise and what you would both like to get from the meeting, e.g. understanding what the other person needs from an ally.
3. Ask the coaching question(s) below.

OR ask your team member to choose a question that they wouldn't like to answer and ask them to explain why. What does this specific question reveal? What thoughts does it prompt in relation to what it is they want to achieve?

Coaching questions:

- What does allyship mean to you, and why is it important in our team environment?
- How can we ensure that everyone feels seen, heard, and valued within the team?
- Can you think of a time when you felt supported by someone? What did that look like?
- How do you currently support others in the team, and where could you improve?
- What are some ways we can create space for voices that are less often heard in meetings or discussions?
- How do you handle situations where someone feels excluded or marginalised? What can you do differently?
- How can you proactively check your biases to ensure inclusivity in your actions and decisions?
- What are some specific actions you can take to demonstrate allyship daily in the workplace?
- How do you approach difficult conversations about inclusion or bias with your colleagues?
- What assumptions do you think you may hold that could impact your ability to be an ally?
- How can you hold yourself accountable for being an active ally in the team?
- How can we create a culture where giving and receiving feedback around inclusivity is normalised and safe?

- In what ways can we celebrate and leverage the diversity within the team?
- What challenges or obstacles have you noticed that might prevent team members from being allies to each other?
- How do you think allyship could improve team performance and collaboration?
- How can you better educate yourself on the experiences of marginalised or underrepresented groups within our team or organisation?
- What support or resources do you need to feel empowered to be a better ally?
- How do you encourage others to speak up or advocate for themselves and others?
- What is one behaviour you can change or adopt today to become a better ally?
- How can we create ongoing opportunities to reflect on and improve our allyship as a team?

FURTHER READING

IT Governance Publishing (ITGP) is the world's leading publisher for governance and compliance. Our industry-leading pocket guides, books and training resources are written by real-world practitioners and thought leaders. They are used globally by audiences of all levels, from students to C-suite executives.

Our high-quality publications cover all IT governance, risk and compliance frameworks and are available in a range of formats. This ensures our customers can access the information they need in the way they need it.

Other publications you may find useful include:

- *Well-being in the Workplace –A guide to resilience for individuals and teams* by Sarah Cook, *www.itgovernance.co.uk/shop/product/well-being-in-the-workplace-a-guide-to-resilience-for-individuals-and-teams*
- *Making a Success of Managing and Working Remotely* by Sarah Cook, *www.itgovernance.co.uk/shop/product/making-a-success-of-managing-and-working-remotely*
- *Mastering Effective Influencing Skills for Win-Win Outcomes – A practical guide* by Sarah Cook, *https://www.itgovernance.co.uk/shop/product/mastering-effective-influencing-skills-for-win-win-outcomes-a-practical-guide*

Further reading

- *An Education in Service Management – A guide to building a successful service management career and delivering organisational success* by David Barrow, *www.itgovernance.co.uk/shop/product/an-education-in-service-management-a-guide-to-building-a-successful-service-management-career-and-delivering-organisational-success*

For more information on ITGP and branded publishing services, and to view our full list of publications, visit *www.itgovernancepublishing.co.uk*.

To receive regular updates from ITGP, including information on new publications in your area(s) of interest, sign up for our newsletter: *www.itgovernancepublishing.co.uk/topic/newsletter.*

Branded publishing

Through our branded publishing service, you can customise ITGP publications with your company's branding.

Find out more at

www.itgovernancepublishing.co.uk/topic/branded-publishing-services.

Related services

ITGP is part of GRC International Group, which offers a comprehensive range of complementary products and services to help organisations meet their objectives.

For a full range of GCR International Group's resources, visit *www.itgovernance.co.uk/*.

Training services

The IT Governance training programme is built on our extensive practical experience designing and implementing management systems based on ISO standards, best practice and regulations.

Our courses help attendees develop practical skills and comply with contractual and regulatory requirements. They also support career development via recognised qualifications.

Learn more about our training courses and view the full course catalogue at *www.itgovernance.co.uk/training*.

Professional services and consultancy

We are a leading global consultancy of IT governance, risk management and compliance solutions. We advise businesses around the world on their most critical issues and present cost-saving and risk-reducing solutions based on international best practice and frameworks.

We offer a wide range of delivery methods to suit all budgets, timescales and preferred project approaches.

Find out how our consultancy services can help your organisation at *www.itgovernance.co.uk/consulting*.

Industry news

Want to stay up to date with the latest developments and resources in the IT governance and compliance market? Subscribe to our Weekly Round-up newsletter and we will send you mobile-friendly emails with fresh news and features about your preferred areas of interest, as well as unmissable offers and free resources to help you successfully start your projects. *www.itgovernance.co.uk/weekly-round-up*.

EU for product safety is Stephen Evans, The Mill Enterprise Hub, Stagreenan, Drogheda, Co. Louth, A92 CD3D, Ireland. (servicecentre@itgovernance.eu)

www.ingramcontent.com/pod-product-compliance
Lightning Source LLC
Chambersburg PA
CBHW042313210326
41599CB00038B/7115